Malakoff Diggins State Historic Park is the site of one of the better known "[...]gins" where huge water powered monitors were used to wash away entire hi[...]in the Forty-Niners' relentless pursuit of gold. This destructive style of mini[...]banned on January 23, 1884, by the Sawyer Decision based on the Anti-Deb[...]of 1883. The effect of hydraulic mining is still seen today in the permanent [...]placement of many rivers in California's gold rush country and the valleys below.

Below, Right. This historic picture illustrates the powerful effect of hydraulic mining at Malakoff Diggins. Courtesy of California Department of Parks and Recreation.

This 1848 drawing of Sutter's Mill shows the tail race where Marshall discovered gold. Courtesy of Marshall Gold Discovery State Historic Park.

CALIFORNIA'S
GOLD RUSH
COUNTRY

Text and photography © 1997 Leslie A. Kelly

Les Kelly Publications
15802 Springdale Street, Suite 14
Huntington Beach, CA 92649-1765
Tel: (714) 846-0437 FAX: (714) 846-8858

Printed and Bound in Hong Kong for
Publishers Print Management Group, Leawood, Kansas
Art Direction by Robert Lynch

Library of Congress Catalog Card Number 96-94597
Kelly, Leslie A., 1940 -
ISBN 0-9653443-0-4

First Edition
1 2 3 4 5 6 7 8 9 0

CALIFORNIA'S GOLD RUSH COUNTRY

Pete Lawson, a member of the gun slinging Jamestown Players, demonstrates gold panning at Wood's Crossing on Wood's Creek near Jamestown, site of the first discovery of gold in Tuolumne County in August 1848.

Contents

Foreword 11
California's Gold Rush Country 12
Coloma: Gold Discovery Site 16
The 49ers: The Way West 24
San Francisco: The Town Built by Gold 52
Sacramento: Sutter's Fort 56
The Northern Mines 62
    Placer County 64
    Nevada County 74
    Sierra County 88
    Plumas County 99
    Yuba County 112
    Sutter County 124
    Butte County 126
    Shasta County 134
    Trinity County 136
    Humboldt County 142
The Southern Mines 144
    El Dorado County 146
    Amador County 152
    Calaveras County 166
    Tuolumne County 182
    Stanislaus County 208
    Mariposa County 210
    Mono County 224
Acknowledgements 227
Appendix 228
Postword 234

Pages 4 - 5: *This early morning scene of the Carson River in Happy Valley, near Carson Pass, depicts the scenic grandeur found in the Sierra Nevada. The Carson Pass was a favored route for many of the 49ers bound for California's gold rush country.*

Pages 6 - 7: *The Fireman's Muster, held each May at Columbia State Historic Park, Site of Columbia, "Gem of the Southern Mines," hosts many fire departments from throughout California's gold rush country. Here, in the 1995 Muster, the Sonora women pump their way to victory over the Sonora men in the long distance competition.*

Above: *At Shasta State Historic Park, Site of Shasta, "Queen City" of the Northern Mines, the Courthouse Museum is highlighted by a colorful rainbow that leads to golden Scotch Broom flowers. Built in 1855 as a commercial building, the Courthouse Museum served as the Shasta County Courthouse from 1861 through 1888. The museum now houses excellent displays from one of the important gold mining and transportation centers in northern California.*

Opposite Page: *Pete Lawson and horse are dwarfed by huge rocks at Columbia, "Gem of the Southern Mines," now preserved as Columbia State Historic Park. The 250 acre wasteland was created by miners who removed the topsoil to a depth of 60 feet in their quest to find gold.*

Spring is a beautiful season in California's gold rush country as depicted by these colorful scenes from Mariposa County.

Foreword

Above: *An idyllic Fall setting on the Mokelumne River near Big Bar is quiet where 150 years ago miners lined the banks seeking the "color" in the river bed.*

Below: *At Rich Bar, the North Fork of the Feather River rages at flood stage rendering all mining impossible during the winter months.*

In the Spring of 1993, while reviewing dates in American history for potential new photo book subjects, I rediscovered California's gold rush. It was an era that I had read about extensively as a youth. I traveled throughout the area as an adult and photographed these locales for travel stories.

On Memorial Day weekend, 1993, accompanied by my children, Erin and Patrick, I visited the area from Mariposa to Placerville to research the possibility of a coffee table book depicting the remnants of California's gold rush era. Thus began what was to become an odyssey of more than forty trips over three years which resulted in this scenic pictorial, **California's Gold Rush Country**.

During my trips to and through California's gold rush country, many people assisted me with information, historic pictures and helped set up current photography. Their assistance was invaluable to the completion of **California's Gold Rush Country**. They include:

Jim Lenhoff, Historian and Author, Oroville; Superintendent Matt Sugarman and Chief Ranger Rosanne Smith McHenry, Marshall Gold Discovery State Historic Park, Coloma; Nancy Sikes, Kelli Coane and Robert "Buzz" Baxter, Tuolumne County Visitors Bureau, Sonora; Tom Bender and Kathi Harvey, The City Hotel, Ranger Sherrin N. Grout, California State Parks, Davy Stoller, Columbia Stage Line & Stable, Columbia State Historic Park, Columbia; and Don Haag, Mariposa County Chamber of Commerce, Mariposa.

Special thanks go to the Crotty Family, Tom, Suzanne, Kathleen, Kevin and Brigid, of Healdsburg, California, and my son Patrick, who, with Chief Ranger Rosanne Smith McHenry, posed for the cover picture at Marshall Gold Discovery State Historic Park; Pete Lawson and Jim "Arthritis" Christensen, Jamestown Players, Jamestown, for their assistance with period pictures at Columbia State Historic Park; and Bill Ventura, Huntington Beach.

Warm thanks are due to my wife, Cathy, for her inspiration and companionship during the years of this project; my mother, Eblene, for her guidance and support over the years; my daughter, Erin, and my son, Patrick, for their assistance with photo selection and proof reading of **California's Gold Rush Country**.

California's Gold Rush Country

This simple entry, written by Henry Bigler in his diary on January 24, 1848, records the momentous discovery of gold at the edge of the South Fork of the American River by James W. Marshall. Bigler, a former member of the famed Mormon Battalion, was one of a few people present at Sutter's Mill in Coloma, when Marshall, "Boss of the Mill," picked up gold nuggets in the tailrace.

Miners came from Australia, Chile, China, England, France, Germany, Italy, Mexico, Panama, Peru, the Sandwich Islands (Hawaii) and "the States" because California did not become the 31st state until 1850. The hordes of argonauts who roamed the rivers, creeks, gulches and canyons of the Sierra Nevada dammed up and virtually dug up all of the rivers and creeks seeking "the color" and quick riches they thought were buried there. They worked feverishly to find their stake!

Much has changed from the days of the gold rush in California's gold rush country. Little remains from the early years when the word "rush" truly characterized the miner's lifestyle. In their haste to find gold, the 49ers only took time to erect tents or simple cabins to provide basic shelter from the elements. On river bars and mountain sides where settlements sprang up and buildings erected, they were often destroyed by fire or collapsed from neglect after the 49ers "rushed" to another reported gold discovery.

Man's mark on nature is still evident in many areas of California's gold rush country after 150 years. Even though the several hundred thousand miners literally dug up all of the rivers and creeks in this area, little remains to mark the sites of hundreds of tent cities that sprang up along the banks and bars of creeks and rivers. Trees and brush have grown back over the banks of the streams. Subsequent floods have washed away many of the huge piles of rocks stacked by the 49ers and restored the stream beds to a natural appearance.

Notable exceptions exist, of course, and none are more striking than Malakoff Diggins in Nevada County and the Spring Valley Mine at Cherokee. Hydraulic mining was an effective way to uncover gold but it was very destructive of the environment. It filled the adjacent rivers with mud, rocks and trees washed away by the huge monitors used in hydraulic mining. Marysville, on the banks of the Yuba River which filled with debris to a depth of 70 feet, and Sacramento, on the banks of the American River, are protected by levees from flooding caused by upriver mining activity. Those who visit Columbia, "Gem of the Southern Mines," marvel at the acres of large rocks that protrude from the ground like silent, gray sentinels. These rocks, exposed by 49ers in their relentless search for gold, were once buried deep beneath the earth.

Few buildings from the early years of California's gold rush remain. Some of those that remain, unfortunately, are in a state of neglect and are in danger of being lost to the ravages of time.

Many of the buildings that remain, however, are preserved and available to tourists to visit. Historic buildings exist principally in Mariposa, Coulterville, Hornitos, Chinese Camp, Groveland, Jamestown, Sonora, Columbia, Angels Camp, Murphys, San Andreas, Mokelumne Hill, Jackson, Sutter Creek, Placerville, Coloma, Auburn, Grass Valley, Nevada City, Downieville, Quincy, Marysville, Oroville and Weaverville. All reflect the varied lifestyles and origin of their builders.

Henry Bigler's diary, "Monday 24th this day some kind of mettle was found in the tail race that looks like goald first discovered by James Martial the Boss of the Mill." Courtesy Jim Lenhoff Collection.

Annie Kelly, left, and Eblene Kelly read the roadside marker at the site of Tuttletown in Tuolumne County. Many such sites are marked only by signs with all traces of buildings and mining activity eradicated by the passage of time.

On a hill high above the South Fork of the American River, California poppies (Eschscholzia californica) paint a peaceful scene less than a mile up river from where James W. Marshall first discovered gold on January 24, 1848.

It is evident from reading the many letters and diaries written by the 49ers that few found their wealth seeking "the color." Mining required standing all day in ice cold water that flowed down from the high Sierra's melting snow pack, sifting tons of dirt in back breaking work while the California sun shone mercilessly from the bright blue sky. Adding to the misery created by the heat and cold water, many diaries tell of long bouts with the "poison oak" illness. Poison oak is still a nuisance for visitors to California's gold rush country.

A major source of revenue in California's gold rush country is found in antiques, not from the gold rush era, but from back East. This store is located at Drytown in Amador County.

Few miners seldom mined enough gold to provide even a meager existence. Indeed, many "saw the elephant" and left penniless to return home. Besides the few lucky miners who made it to the rivers in '48 and '49, the majority of those made wealthy by the gold rush were the merchants who sold food, supplies and other services to the miners at exorbitantly high prices.

Not even the two men associated with the discovery of gold at Sutter's Mill on January 24, 1848, profited. James W. Marshall, who found the first flakes in the tail race at Sutter's Mill on that fateful day, died a bitter and penniless man. John Sutter, whose dream of New Helvetia was crushed by the rush of 49ers to the rivers and creeks on his lands, wrote in a letter to J. M. Hutchings, published in Hutchings' California Magazine, November 1857: *"By this sudden discovery of the gold, all my great plans were destroyed. Had I succeeded with my mills and manufactories for a few years before the gold was discovered, I should have been the richest citizen on the Pacific shore; but it had to be different. Instead of being rich, I am ruined."*

A number of men who participated in the gold rush did go on to become successful businessmen, for example, Levi Strauss, Studebaker, Ghirardelli, Crocker, Macy, Stanford, Bidwell and Hearst.

Perhaps the most important group of people to follow the 49ers at the end of California's gold rush were those who sought to preserve its history, its buildings and sites, for those who now commemorate California's gold rush sesquicentennial. These preservationists include individual descendants of pioneers, numerous city and county historical societies, the California Historical Society (1871), the Native Sons of the Golden West (1875) and the Native Daughters of the Golden West (1886). The California Centennial Commission was active in 1949, placing many markers at historic sites. Today, the E Clampus Vitus is active in marking historic sites in California's gold rush country. A number of California State Parks, notable are the Marshall Gold Discovery State Historic Park, Columbia State Historic Park, the Sutter's Fort State Historic Park and Malakoff Diggins State Historic Park, preserve historic sites for all to visit and to appreciate the historic significance of California's gold rush.

California's Gold Rush Country generally covers the years from 1848 through 1858. The rush for gold began in 1848 and tapered off a few years later. It began anew in 1855 and ended in 1858 with the discovery of silver at the Comstock Mine in Nevada City, Nevada. California remained an important gold mining region with the advent of hard rock mining.

The mining areas of California's gold rush country are divided into the Southern Mines, those south of Auburn, and the Northern Mines, those located north of Auburn. **California's Gold Rush Country** begins at Coloma, where it all began, and moves geographically north to Humboldt County and then returns to cover the areas south to Mariposa County. California's Mother Lode Country, named for the one hundred mile long vein of gold bearing quartz believed to be buried in the Sierra Nevada, extends from Mariposa to Nevada County. Also included are the California Overland Trail from Independence, Missouri, the major land route to California, the Panama Isthmus, which played a major role in the sea route to San Francisco and the better known hard rock mines that followed the gold rush.

The majority of California's gold rush country is either directly on or not far from California Highway 49. This highway was named in honor of the 49ers who made the gold rush what it became, a rush of humanity seeking to make a fortune by picking up rumored fist-sized nuggets from the creeks and rivers of the area.

The hordes of argonauts who roamed the rivers, creeks, gulches and canyons seeking "the color" have been replaced by throngs of tourists, motorcyclists, bicyclists and antique car enthusiasts. All yearn to capture the feeling of a distant time in which they were not privileged to participate. While travel was simple at that time, even with modern highways and the encroachment of civilization at the approach of the 21st Century, it is possible to drive through most gold rush era towns with not even a stop sign, let alone a traffic light, to slow vehicles.

Whether the reader is a visitor to California's gold rush country or settles into a soft chair for an armchair tour, please enjoy this look at the beauty of what remains 150 years after the rush to and through California's gold fields.

Opposite Page, Above, Right. Wells, Fargo and Company's office at Columbia in the 1870's. Courtesy Wells Fargo Bank.

Opposite Page, Below, Left. Telegraph Hill in San Francisco is portrayed early in the gold rush. The telegraph building on top on the hill was used to signal the arrival of ships; around about are tents of 49ers. Courtesy Wells Fargo Bank.

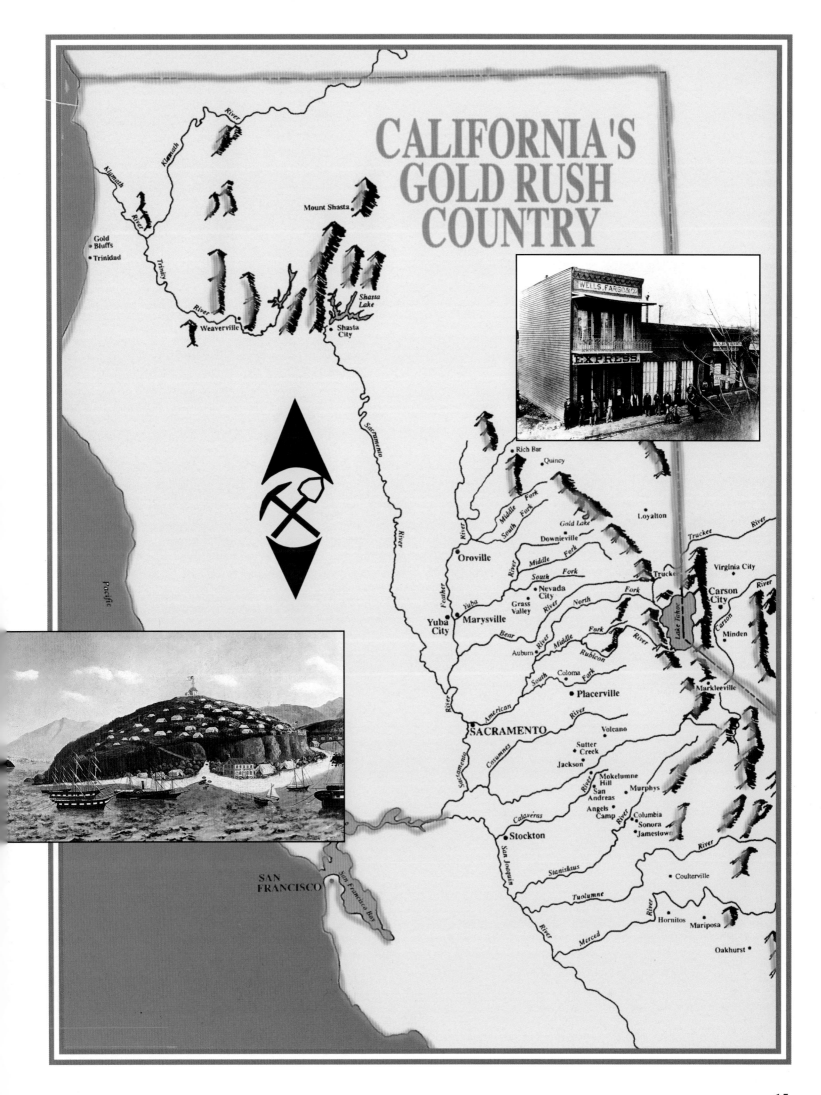

CALIFORNIA'S GOLD RUSH COUNTRY

Klamath River

Klamath River

Trinity River

Gold Bluffs

Trinidad

Mount Shasta

River

Weaverville

Shasta Lake

Shasta City

Sacramento River

WELLS, FARGO & CO.
EXPRESS

Rich Bar

Quincy

Middle Fork
South Fork

Gold Lake

Loyalton

Downieville

Truckee River

Oroville

River

Middle Fork

South Fork

Nevada City

Fork

North Fork

Virginia City

Feather River

Yuba River

Grass Valley

River

Truckee

Carson City

River

Yuba City

Marysville

Fork

Lake Tahoe

Minden

Bear River

Auburn

Middle Fork

Rubicon

Fork

Carson River

South Fork

Coloma

Markleeville

Sacramento River

American River

Placerville

River

Volcano

SACRAMENTO

Cosumnes River

Sutter Creek

Jackson

Mokelumne Hill

San Andreas

Murphys

River

Angels Camp

Columbia

Sonora

Jamestown

Calaveras River

Stockton

San Joaquin River

Stanislaus River

Coulterville

River

Tuolumne River

SAN FRANCISCO

San Francisco Bay

Hornitos

Mariposa

Merced River

Oakhurst

Pacific

Coloma, Queen of the Mines

The South Fork of the American River has changed its course since Sutter first directed the building of his and Marshall's sawmill here.   The tailrace exit into the river, however, is still visible.

James W. Marshall was born in New Jersey on October 8, 1810. He grew up in Lambertville, a short distance from where George Washington made his celebrated crossing of the Delaware. Marshall gained experience as a carpenter and worked in sawmills along the east coast until he joined one of the wagon trains bound for Oregon in 1844. In 1845, he arrived at Sutter's Fort and was immediately employed by John Sutter. When the Bear Flag Rebellion broke out in 1847, he participated in the relief effort to secure Sonoma. He left Sutter and joined the Battalion of California Volunteers with which he served until the end of war with Mexico. He rejoined Sutter as a partner and began work on the sawmill project on the North Fork of the American River. It was in his role as "Boss of the Mill" that Marshall found a permanent place in world history.

The sites of Marshall's discovery and of Coloma and its remaining historic buildings have been incorporated into the 273 acre Marshall Gold Discovery State Historic Park.

This small channel was the outlet of the tailrace where Marshall found gold.

Visitors to Coloma and the Marshall Gold Discovery State Historic Park find an excellent Museum and Visitor Center. A well marked self-guided tour of the park allows visitors to leisurely view buildings and displays from an era when man's rush to find gold here created a town overnight. Indeed, many miners passed through Coloma, much as tourists do today, to see where it all began and say that they were there! Only some 600 to 900 residents called Coloma home during the height of the gold rush. In 1850, when El Dorado County was formed, Coloma became the county seat.

Above. Visitors entering the Marshall Gold Discovery State Historic Park from the south on Highway 49 pass by the renovated schoolhouse built in 1919. *Center, Right.* Only walls remain of the once popular Bell Store which dates to 1855. *Below.* The Episcopal Church, built in 1855, is one of the most prominent buildings from historic Coloma.

Above. Freight wagons like these were used to haul freight overland throughout California's gold rush country during the gold rush era. In the background are two stone buildings, left, partially obscured, the Wah Hop building and, right, the Man Lee Store building. Both date to the late 1850s and are all that remain of Coloma's Chinatown.

Center, Left. The Man Lee Store now houses interpretive displays. The Chinatown at Coloma was one of the largest in California's gold rush country.

Center, Right. The historic Coloma Cemetery is located on a hillside south of Coloma.

Below. The replica of Sutter's Mill stands near the site of the original sawmill. Nearby is a replica of the Mormon Cabin used to house Mormon workers who were employed by Marshall to construct a sawmill for Marshall and Sutter.

The Marshall Gold Discovery State Historic Park is the site of the annual National Gold Panning Championships. Attracting participants from all over the world, activities are held at the edge of the South Fork of the American River.

Above. A raised pan stops the clock for this competition winner.

Center, Left. Blacksmithing is demonstrated by Bill Curry (left) and Tom Bartlett .

Center, Right. Musicians provide period entertainment for visitors.

Below, Left. Monica Woods, KTXL-TV, Channel 40, Sacramento television personality, displays her panning techniques during the celebrity event.

Below, Center. A Swedish competitor displays her gold strike for the camera.

Below, Right. The historic Bekeart's Gunshop, built in 1854 by Frank Bekeart, is the third such shop operated on this site.

The Museum at Marshall Gold Discovery State Historic Park provides excellent displays that explain how gold was formed and how it was mined. Period artifacts provide an excellent view of Sutter's Mill and James W. Marshall's life in Coloma.

A number of displays include artist sketches and early pictures of Sutter's Mill and Coloma.

One of the most interesting exhibits in the Museum is the timber from the original mill recovered during an archeological investigation in 1947.

Various pieces of mining equipment are on display on the grounds of the Museum.

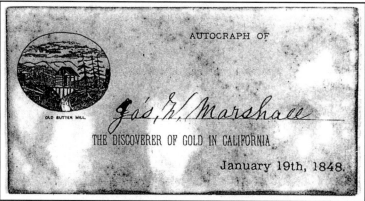

When James W. Marshall died on August 10, 1885, he was buried on the hill overlooking the site where he first discovered gold. In 1890, this statue commemorating his discovery of gold was erected over his grave site. It was only after his death that Marshall received praise and accolades from those who benefited from his discovery of gold at Sutter's Mill.

Above, Right. James Marshall was 37, in 1848, soon after he found gold at Sutter's Mill, when this portrait by H. Eastman was completed. Courtesy of Marshall Gold Discovery State Historic Park.

Center, Left. Although Marshall was given credit for discovery of gold at Sutter's Mill in the official government report prepared by Colonel Richard B. Mason, Marshall never did profit from his discovery of gold. After 1848, he spent a number of years prospecting for gold, all without significant success.

In his latter years, Marshall sold his signature and this card for 25¢ to the curious who sought him out for advice on prospecting gold. Courtesy of Marshall Gold Discovery State Historic Park.

Below, Left. In 1857, Marshall lived in a cabin on the hillside above Coloma. He planted a vineyard and worked as a carpenter. When the cabin burned in 1862, Marshall rebuilt it where it stands today, near the St. John's Catholic Church.

Below, Right. Only the walls remain from this museum building which housed Marshall's blacksmith shop built in 1872-73 at Kelsey. Its contents were removed to Sutter's Fort State Historic Park in Sacramento. Marshall worked two small claims near Kelsey, the Gray Eagle and the Big Sandy, and lived in a small room at the Union Hotel at Kelsey until his death.

At the height of the gold rush, the South Fork of the American River was crowded with miners seeking "the color." Today, it is filled with thrill seekers in colorful rubber rafts and kayaks.

The 49ers: The Way West

California first came to the attention of Europeans in 1542 when the Spanish explorer Juan Rodriguez Cabrillo sailed the length of its coast. He was followed by Sir Francis Drake in 1579 who claimed California for England. Sebastián Vizcaíno's voyages in the early 1600s resulted in the naming of most of the landmarks along the California coast.

When Spain became concerned about England's intentions in the area, it began land explorations in 1769 that led to the colonization of Alta California. Presidios were established at the sea ports of San Francisco, Monterey, Santa Barbara and San Diego, and pueblos (towns) at Los Angeles and San José. A chain of twenty-one missions, built a day's ride apart, extended from San Diego to Sonoma. Their efforts led to the colonization and creation of an agricultural empire throughout Alta California. When Mexico achieved independence from Spain in 1821, it encouraged agricultural pursuits in the region.

Early American explorers made their way west to California in the early 1800s. Their excursions into Alta California were generally peaceful. Most of these explorers were fur trappers, traders, scouts and adventurers who became well known for their role in opening up the west to migration and permanent settlement. They include Jedediah Strong Smith, John C. Frémont, Kit Carson, Jim Bridger, James Beckwourth and Joseph Reddeford Walker.

The way west from the United States to California began as a trickle in 1841. Thirty-two members of the Bidwell-Bartleson Party, led by General John Bidwell, completed the first migration whose purpose was to settle in California.

Pioneer Wagon, Fort Kearny, Nebraska

Below, Right. Gold on American River!
On March 15, 1848, this small notice was printed in the Californian on page three. It was ignored as being just another false claim that gold had been found. Courtesy Jim Lenhoff Collection.

Below, Left. *This map on display in the National Frontier Trails Center at Independence, Missouri, graphically illustrates the way west. Strategically located on the Missouri River at the western edge of the United States, Independence was the main jumping off point for 49ers bound for California.*

In 1843, "The Great Migration" occurred when some 1,000 people used wagons to reach Oregon. While the Bear Flag Rebellion of 1846 led to control of California by General Stephen W. Kearny, the American military governor, it was not until news reached the east coast that gold was discovered at Sutter's Mill that migration west began in earnest.

Those already in California were able to search for gold immediately. Only a few hundred people responded when word reached the east coast on April 15, 1848. The real rush began when President James K. Polk, in his annual message to Congress, wrote on December 5, 1848:

"The accounts of abundance of gold are of such an extraordinary character, as would scarcely command belief were they not corroborated by the authentic reports of officers in the public service."

Gold fever swept "the States." The rush was on! The way west by land required planning and preparation for the six month trip. Grass had to green up to feed the horses and cattle and the sturdy oxen used to pull the heavy wagons. Those making the trek had to depart in April or May from Independence, Missouri, the last town before the prairie and Indian Territory at the western edge of the United States.

Gold fever increased from a trickle to a rush in 1849 when an estimated 90,000 miners arrived in California. By land and by sea, miners rushed west to claim their share of wealth. No matter which year they went west, whether 1849, 1850 or 1852, they were all called 49ers!

CALIFORNIAN
BY B. R. BUCKELEW

SAN FRANCISCO, MARCH 15, 1848

The LIBERTY of the Press, consists in the right to publish the TRUTH, with good motives and for justifiable ends —ALEX HAMILTON

——ooo——

GOLD MINE FOUND.—In the newly made raceway of the Saw Mill recently erected by Captain Sutter, on the American Fork, gold has been found in considerable quantities. One person brought thirty dollars worth to New Helvetia, gathered there in a short time. California, no doubt, is rich in mineral wealth, great chances here for scientific capitalists. Gold has been found in almost every part of the country.

The most common land route used by the 49ers to get to California, began at Independence, Missouri, and ended some 2,000 miles and six months later at Johnson's Crossing, near Wheatland, in Yuba County. The way west was arduous and many died along the trail.

Because stories of depredations by Indians were common, many of the 49ers departed for California armed to the teeth. This heavy armament led to more self-inflicted wounds (and resultant death) than from attacks by Indians along the trail.

The most serious risk faced by the 49ers on their way west came from cholera. In late 1848, cholera spread from Europe to New York and New Orleans. According to Dr. Roger P. Blair, MD., Sheridan, Wyoming, at the time when the 49ers were preparing to travel to California by land and by sea, the cholera epidemic was spreading across the United States, across the California Overland Trail and the sea routes. Between 1849 and 1885, the cholera epidemic killed untold thousands on the trail and at sea.

The California Overland Trail paralleled the Oregon Trail to Idaho. From there, it branched off and led southwest across Nevada. For those who had already traveled almost 2,000 miles across prairie and mountains, the 40 Mile Desert at the end of the Nevada crossing proved to be a real hardship. No water, no grass and blinding white alkali pools took their toll on humans and animals alike. Finally, only the steep walls of the Sierra Nevada remained before them. By sheer force of their numbers, courage and determination, this once formidable wall of granite was crossed and California was opened to westward migration.

By sea, the distance was considerably longer, depending on whether the route was around Cape Horn at the southern tip of South America, or involved transit across the Isthmus of Panama. The later route proved to be the easiest and was often favored over the land route for the return trip home by Americans.

By 1858, more than 600,000 men, women and children made their way west to join in California's gold rush. Most came for the gold and returned home. Many, however, stayed on to develop the Golden State into a major economic and political force in the USA.

Alcove Springs, near Blue Rapids, Kansas was considered by many to be the most romantic spot along the trail. The Donner Party carved "Alcove Springs" on a rock, which is still visible today, when they camped here in May 1846 prior to meeting their fate in the snows of the Sierra Nevada.

Emigrants and 49ers alike found present day Kansas to be a good proving ground for their oxen and wagons. The flat land and gentle rivers helped prepare them for the perilous trip ahead.

Above. *The historic Hollenberg Ranch house was built about 1857 on the Oregon-California Trail near Hanover, Kansas. In 1860, Hollenberg Ranch became a station for the short lived Pony Express. According to Duane Durst, Curator, Hollenberg Pony Express Station is the only remaining station in its original location.*

Center, Left. *Rick Pralle, left, and Ronald Holle demonstrate the passing of the mochilla, the Pony Express mail pouch, at Hollenberg Pony Express Station.*

Below. *Fort Kearny, named in honor of General Stephen Watts Kearny, hero of the Mexican War and first military governor of California, was established in 1848 to protect emigrants on their way west. It is located near Kearney, Nebraska.*

Above. *The Platte River, known as the Great Platte River Road, was often described by emigrants as being a mile wide and an inch deep. This sunset scene at Alda, Nebraska, is near the point where The Oregon-California Trail met the Platte River. Emigrants and 49ers followed it and the North Platte as far west as Fort Caspar, Wyoming. It served as a guide for all and provided a natural barrier for the Mormon emigrants, who generally followed the north side to Fort Laramie, Wyoming, and "the Gentiles" who generally stayed on the south side. The Mormons departed from Council Bluffs, Iowa, with Salt Lake City as their destination.*

Nebraska provided the first real challenge for emigrants and 49ers with hills and river crossings. Many emigrant diaries noted that the prairie crossing was boring. However, the sight of some of America's most unique landmarks helped break the monotony.

Left. Windlass Hill, near Ash Hollow, was the steepest hill encountered in Nebraska along the Oregon-California Trail. Deep ruts mark the steep descent followed by the wagons.

Center. Ancient Ruins Bluffs, near Lisco, Nebraska were named by the Mormon emigrants from Europe who found their shape similar to castle ruins in their native lands. These formations are on the North side of the Platte River.

Below. On the south side of the Platte, Courthouse and Jail House Rocks were the first of several natural landmarks passed between Bridgeport and Scotts Bluff. Many climbed these rocks for a view of the surrounding prairie or to carve their name in the soft sides of Brule clay.

Above. At Gering, Nebraska, the castellated bluffs of Scotts Bluff and Mitchell Pass, within the Scotts Bluff National Monument, dominate the western end of the Gering Valley.

Right. Covered wagons depict the historic theme of Scotts Bluff National Monument. The nearby visitor's center houses an excellent museum and collection of trail memorabilia.

Below. Silhouetted by a vivid sunset, Chimney Rock —a few miles west of Courthouse and Jail House Rocks at Bayard —was the landmark most often noted by emigrants in their diaries.

Center. William Henry Jackson, a teamster on the Oregon Trail and one of the better known artists of the era, drew this view of the valley from Chimney Rock to Scotts Bluff at a point near Bridgeport. Courtesy Scotts Bluff National Monument.

Many emigrants and 49ers kept diaries which provide historians with rich sources of information about their life along the Oregon-California Trail and the California gold rush. Artists, among those who traveled west, provided graphic depiction of life on the trail and sketches of landmarks.

Left. This unusual reflection view of Chimney Rock, taken at 5:15 a.m., was the result of local flooding after heavy thunderstorms overnight.

Center. Sketches by William Quesenbury, a native of Arkansas who joined in the California gold rush, include a view similar to that of Jackson. This sketch of Chimney Rock, labeled "Distant view from the East," is one of several important sketches he made in 1851 as he returned home to Arkansas from the gold fields of California. *Courtesy Omaha World-Herald Quesenbury Sketchbook.*

Below. This contemporary scene was photographed from the approximate site used by Jackson and Quesenbury for their sketches. The Nebraska State Historical Society operates the Chimney Rock Visitor Center near Bayard. It houses an excellent collection of drawings and photography depicting the history of Chimney Rock.

31

Left. These ruts in the sandstone rock at Deep Ruts Hill near Guernsey, Wyoming, are a vivid reminder of the tens of thousands of wagons that rolled though this area.

Above. Fort Laramie played a significant role as a source of supplies and repairs for damaged equipment for emigrants and 49ers. It was first established by the American Fur Company and later purchased in 1849 by the U. S. government. It was here that the Mormons joined trails with the other emigrants in their trek West to Salt Lake City.

Below. Fort Caspar at Casper, Wyoming, marked the point where emigrants left the North Platte behind and began their climb into the Rockies. A replica of the ferry operated by the Mormons is shown here.

Independence Rock, alongside the Sweetwater River, was given its name by fur trappers who camped here on July 4, 1824 or from William Sublette who camped there on July 4, 1830. Emigrants tried to arrive here on the same date. It was named the "register of the desert" by Father Pierre DeSmet, a pioneer missionary. Most who passed here climbed to the top for an excellent view of the surrounding land. Many — estimated at more than 40,000 — etched their name with axle grease or chisel in the soft limestone of Independence Rock.

Inset. Thousands of names, such as that of J. J. Hughes who visited on July 4, 1850, can still be seen.

Singularly the most important of all of the landmarks along the Oregon-California Trail, South Pass, Wyoming, a virtually flat crossing of the continental divide at 7,550 feet, is perhaps the least prominent in features. Emigrants made note in their diaries that its twenty nine mile width and gradual ascent were so gentle that they sometimes didn't notice that they had crossed the divide. At Pacific Springs, just west of South Pass, they found the first waters to flow west. The snowcapped Wind River Range, to the north, adds to the desolate beauty of this important pass.

Inset. Ezra Meeker, an Oregon emigrant of 1852, placed this marker "Old Oregon Trail 1843-57" here in 1906. At age 75, he made the first of three covered wagon trips from Oregon to Independence to encourage preservation of the Oregon Trail.

Above. Mormons operated the important Lombard Ferry that crossed the Green River at this site in Western Wyoming.

Below. Emigrants usually had few kind words to write about Fort Bridger even though they found welcome supplies here. The first fort was built in 1843 by Jim Bridger at another location. The current site, selected in 1844 by Bridger, is set in a scenic valley partially surrounded by the mountains of the Uinta and Wasatch. This replica fort is near remnants of the recon- structed Ft. Bridger, now a Wyoming State Historic Park. The original fort was bought by the Mormons in 1853. They burned the fort to keep it from falling into control of the United States Army during the so-called Mormon War of 1857. During the summer months, the fort is staffed by volunteers who recreate an atmosphere like that of its earlier days. Fort Bridger was the point where the Mormons turned south to go to Salt Lake City. Forty- niners also used the route through Salt Lake City and then northwest to join the California Trail at the City of Rocks, Idaho. Fort Bridger was a fateful stop for the Donner Party. It was here that Lansford Hastings promised — but failed — to meet the party and take them west from Salt Lake City across the Great Salt Lake Desert to the Truckee River.

Opposite Page, Above. In Idaho, the emigrants along the Oregon- California Trail traveled through the Bear River Valley seen here near Georgetown. At Soda Springs, many took a new shortcut to the gold fields on the Hudspeth Cutoff. Rather than continue north to Fort Hall, they head- ed due west for the City of the Rocks and the California Trail.

Opposite Page, Center. The replica of Fort Hall at Pocatello, Idaho, is rem- iniscent of its heyday as an important fur trading post and later as sanctuary for emigrants along the Oregon-California Trail. West of Pocatello, along the Snake River, emigrants followed the Oregon Trail west to the rich

Williamette Valley. At the Raft River, near the Junction of present day I-84 and I-86, the 49ers followed the California Trail south.

Below, Left. Near Almo, Idaho, the California Trail passed directly through the City of Rocks, the area named for the many rocks, some of which are 60-70 stories high, that resemble a silent city. Here, the Twin Sisters Rock marks the junction of the Salt Lake Alternate Trail with the California Trail.

Below, Right. A brilliant sunset colors the sky above the City of Rocks National Preserve. It is jointly administered by the National Park Service and the Idaho Department of Parks and Recreation.

While only a few Mormons participated in the gold rush, their westward migration to Zion occurred during the time of the gold rush by the 49ers. Many provided services along the way, i.e., ferry crossings and for those who travelled through Salt Lake City, fresh horses, oxen and other supplies.

Above. This Is The Place Monument at the mouth of Emigration Canyon celebrates the selection of the Valley of the Great Salt Lake by Brigham Young on July 24, 1847, as the new home for the Mormons. Heber C. Kimball, (left), Young, (center), and Wilford Woodruff, (right), look down upon Salt Lake City. Photo by Leslie A. Kelly courtesy of This is the Place State Park, Utah Division of Parks and Recreation, Department of Natural Resources.

Below, Left. Emigration Canyon, as seen, from Little Mountain, shows the last few miles of the Mormon Trail. Its steep descent was a final test of endurance for those who made the trek into Salt Lake City.

From Idaho, the 49ers followed the Humboldt River west to the Carson Sink where the river's waters disappear into the desert sands. This route closely parallels present day I-80. Before reaching the eastern walls of the Sierra Mountains, the 49ers crossed the Forty Mile Desert. Many abandoned cherished possessions and even wagons as they lightened their loads to increase their chances of safe passage. Animals died of thirst or from water tainted by alkaline deposits.

Some 49ers turned northwest to northern California on the Applegate or Lassen Trail that branched off the California Trail near present day Imley. This route was considered easier by some but was much longer than the Truckee River route which most followed south along the Humboldt River to the Great Meadows or Carson Sink. Here the 49ers had two choices as they crossed the Forty Mile Desert. Due west, along the present day route of I-80, was the Truckee River. Southwest, along the route near Fallon, was the Carson River.

Above. *The California Trail passed through the foreground of this setting near the Carson Sink on the way to the Carson River.*

Right. *A half-moon rises above an alkaline pond along the California Trail near the Carson Sink. Many 49ers traveled across the Forty Mile Desert by moonlight to escape the heat of day.*

41

The Donner Party tragedy weighed heavily upon the minds of the 49ers as they rushed west, eager to beat the snows of the Sierra Nevada that trapped the Donner Party in 1846.

Above. Donner Lake is covered with ice and buried under snow, conditions similar to those encountered by the Donner Party when heavy snows began on October 28, 1846, one month earlier than usual. Donner Pass is in the center of the mountains in the distance.

Left. The Pioneer Monument at Donner Memorial State Park, at Truckee, is dedicated to the 35 who died and the 47 who survived the brutal conditions at Donner Lake during the winter of 1846-47. The base of the monument is 22 feet high, the same as the level of snow that trapped the party. The Pioneer Monument is adjacent to the Donner Memorial State Park Museum. The Museum is distinguished by an excellent interpretive center.

Opposite Page, Above. The peaceful Carson River flows through Hope Valley named by the members of the Mormon Battalion as they departed from California in 1848 to meet their families in Salt Lake City.

Opposite page, Center, Left. Summer flowers and aspens cover the mountains at Carson Pass. The Pass is named for the famed scout and guide, Kit Carson, who first crossed it in February 1844.

Opposite Page, Center, Right. Aspen trees are colored by fall foliage at Carson Pass.

Opposite Page, Below. The Mormon Emigrant Trail, followed west by the 49ers, was carved out of the wilderness by the Mormon Battalion in June 1848 as they traveled from California to Salt Lake City. Here it is seen as a line moving to the right from Red Lake just below Carson Pass.

43

Above. The Mormon Trail passed along the ridge above Silver Lake.

Center, Left. Tragedy Springs was the site where three members of the Mormon Battalion were murdered by Indians on June 27, 1848. Oregon-California Trail Association member Norine Kimmy and son Brian of San Jose, California, pause to contemplate the scene.

Below, Left. Kirkwood Station, built in 1861, was originally a stage stop along the Mormon Trail. It is now a popular stop for snow skiers.

The key to penetration of California's formidable Sierra Nevada range was its passes.

Opposite Page, Above. Beckwourth Pass is named for James Beckwourth, a famous Black scout and trapper, who discovered this easy crossing of the Sierra Nevada — at just 5,212 feet — north of modern day Reno in 1851. The Beckwourth Trail route led to Marysville.

Opposite Page, Center. The Walker River route, named for Joseph Reddeford Walker who also discovered Tioga Pass in 1833, led to the Sonora Pass.

Opposite Page, Below. Henness Pass, which ran along the Yuba River Ridge, was favored by those destined for Nevada City.

Above. The stern paddle wheel riverboat, The Natchez, departs the dock in New Orleans, reminiscent of gold rush era days. Many 49ers took riverboats from New Orleans to Independence, Missouri, to travel by land to California. Others took schooners from New York and New Orleans around Cape Horn or crossed the Isthmus of Panama to get to San Francisco.

Center. President Polk's report to Congress on December 5, 1848, confirmed that gold had been found in California. In this 1850 drawing by William Mount, excited Easterners read the December 9, 1848, edition of The New York Daily Tribune. Horace Greeley wrote: "The perilous stuff lies loose upon the surface of the ground or only slightly adheres to rocks and sand. The only machinery necessary . . . is a stout pair of arms, a shovel and a tin pan." Courtesy Melville Collection, Suffolk Museum & Carriage House.

Opposite Page, Above. Demand was so great for passage to California's gold fields that every ship, brig, schooner or sloop that was half fit to go to sea was pressed into service. In this setting, the steam packet Hartford leaves the East River pier in New York on February 20, 1849, bound for San Francisco. Courtesy Museum of the City of New York.

Opposite Page, Center. Nathaniel Currier drew this humorous look at the rush for the gold fields of California by Easterners.

Opposite Page, Below. San Francisco was the destination of all sea borne 49ers. San Francisco, originally called Yerba Buena, had only a few hundred residents when gold was discovered in 1848. This picture, taken in 1850, shows a sea of ship masts. Hundreds of boats were abandoned upon arriving in San Francisco by their crews which then rushed to the gold fields. Courtesy The Bancroft Library, University of California-Berkeley.

. VIEW OF THE CITY OF CHAGRES.

The Río Chagres played a key role in the crossing of the Isthmus of Panama by 49ers bound for the gold fields. Travel across the Isthmus to Panama City by bungo boat and donkeys took several perilous days. This view of the mouth of Río Chagres and Atlantic Ocean was taken from Fort San Lorenzo built by the Spaniards beginning in 1595. Many of those who made the crossing wrote about the incessant rain. However, of the 60 mile Isthmus Crossing, Bayard Taylor wrote in 1850: "It was decidedly more novel, grotesque and adventurous than any trip of similar length in the world. It had nothing that I could exactly call hardship, so much was the fatigue balanced by the enjoyment of unsurpassed scenery and a continued sensation of novelty." One out of four 49ers traveled to California via the Isthmus. Most who returned home to the east coast did so via the Panama crossing.

The village of Chagres was located at the mouth of the Río Chagres on the Atlantic Coast of Panamá. Here 49ers disembarked from steamers and hired bungo boats (dugouts, usually three feet wide by 25 feet long with a thatch-covered cargo area) to be poled and paddled by natives up river to the town of Gorgona. This journey usually took three days. Courtesy Panama Canal Commission.

From Gorgona the 49ers crossed by land along the Camino de Las Cruces, a trail first built and paved with cobblestones by the Spaniards in the early 1500s. The Spaniards used the trail to transport gold from Panama City to the town of Nombre de Dios where it was taken to Spain. Today, the cobblestones are covered over by growth from the jungle. This portion of the trail is maintained as part of the Parque Nacional de Soberanía.

The town of Chagres and the Río Chagres were abandoned as a route across the Isthmus when the railroad was completed in 1855. Courtesy Panama Canal Commission.

Tourists today can bargain with natives for souvenirs or food as did the 49ers.

The slow moving sloth is but one of many species of animals that the 49ers were certain to have spotted as they traveled through the jungle. This sloth left the trees of the jungle to cross the highway near Fort San Lorenzo.

Americans built a railroad across the Isthmus in 1854. This shortened the time for 49ers to cross the Isthmus from several days to a matter of hours. Some 60 years later, Americans completed the Panama Canal, truly one of the greatest engineering feats in history. Here the Hamlet Saudi with a load of cars and containers approaches the Miraflores Locks on the Pacific (western entrance) side of the Panama Canal.

The skyline of Panama City today reflects a bustling city filled with history.

The Kapitan Vakula, in the company of several tug boats, moves through the first lock on its transit northbound through the Panama Canal.

Táboga Island was used by Pacific Steamship Lines as its port for Panama City. Courtesy Panama Canal Commission.

The ruins of Panamá Vieja were among the sights to be seen by the argonauts on their journey to the gold fields. Founded in 1519 by Spaniards, Panama City served as the storage point for Peruvian gold before it was transported to the Caribbean and Spain. Panamá Vieja was abandoned in 1671 after being sacked by the infamous pirate Henry Morgan.

The Golden Gate Bridge, is partially shrouded by fog, while Alcatraz Island shines in the sun.
The view of the surrounding hills and bays from Telegraph Hill is magnificent.

Reminiscent of gold rush days, schooners line the dock in San Francisco.

Telegraph Hill is partially masked by the Golden Gate Bridge seen here just before sunset.

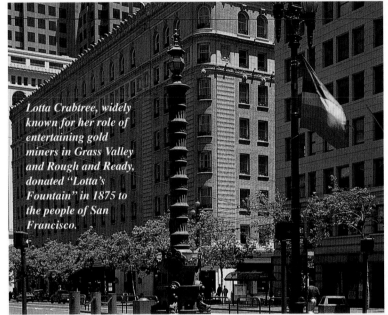

Lotta Crabtree, widely known for her role of entertaining gold miners in Grass Valley and Rough and Ready, donated "Lotta's Fountain" in 1875 to the people of San Francisco.

San Francisco

San Francisco is known as the town built by gold in recognition of its pivotal role during California's gold rush. It served as point of departure for 49ers who came by sea for the gold mines and for their return home. It was the major port of entrance for miners and mining supplies. The majority of the 49ers elected to return home by sea and departed from the Port of San Francisco. The Port was one of the busiest in the world during the gold rush. The San Francisco Mint processed much of the gold found in California for shipment by sea to the east coast. It was Juan Bautista de Anza's expedition of 1774, which opened a land route to northern California, that led to the selection of the site for the Presidio of San Francisco. When Mexico took over Alta California in 1821, agricultural development was encouraged throughout the region. Port activity developed at the cove that became known as Yerba Buena to support the trade of cattle hides. Yerba Buena was changed to San Francisco on March 10, 1847, by General Stephen W. Kearny, the military governor.

Coit Tower on Telegraph Hill, shaped like a fire nozzle in honor of San Francisco's firemen, was erected in 1933 with funds provided by Mrs. Lillie Hitchcock Coit.

A number of major US companies based in San Francisco had their beginnings in California's gold rush.

Above and Left. Domingo Ghirardelli came to California from Italy in 1849 by way of Perú. After an unsuccessful stint panning for gold, he opened a general store at Hornitos (See Page 216) which he operated until 1852. From this time until his death in 1894, Ghirardelli produced his delightful chocolate in San Francisco. The famous Ghirardelli Square celebrates his role in San Francisco's early history and the Ghirardelli Chocolate Company continues his successful chocolate production today. Original equipment used by Ghirardelli is on display.

Opposite Page, Above.   San Francisco's cable cars are an important tourist draw to this corner across from Ghirardelli Square and near Fisherman's Wharf.

Opposite Page, Right, Center. Henry Wells (founder of Wells & Company) and William G. Fargo (Livingston & Fargo, and Butterfield, Wasson & Co.) joined forces in 1850 as American Express Company. In 1852, they moved west to form Wells, Fargo & Company. Their agents played an integral role in banking and transporting gold during the gold rush. The trust of these Wells, Fargo & Company agents is legendary. Wells, Fargo & Company stagecoach driver, Hank Monk, best of those on the Placerville Road, was immortalized in Mark Twain's **Roughing It.** *A number of the historic buildings which served as Wells, Fargo & Company offices have survived and are featured in* **California's Gold Rush Country.** *American Express, whose credit cards and traveler's checks are accepted throughout California's gold rush country and the world, and Wells Fargo & Company, a major force in California's and the world's banking community and economy today, rank among the largest in their respective fields.*

Opposite Page, Right, Below. Boudin Bakery's sourdough bread, first served in San Francisco in 1849 by Isodore Boudin, is still baked fresh daily from flour, salt, water and the original mother dough that dates to the first loaf. Many consider San Francisco sourdough to be the culinary by-product of California's gold rush.

Opposite Page, Left. Levi Strauss sewed heavy cotton fabric to provide miners with rugged clothing suitable to mining in California in 1850. In this picture, dated 1882, the trademark Levi style is easily recognized. Courtesy Levi Strauss & Company

Last Chance Mine
er County, Calif. 1882
BLUE EYES MINE

Sutter's Fort

John Augustus Sutter, an emigrant from Switzerland, arrived in California in July 1839, with grandiose schemes and plans to establish a colony. In August, he settled in what was to become Sacramento. Here he built a fort, Sutter's Fort, and called the settlement New Helvetia. In 1841, when the Russian settlement at Fort Ross was closed, he bought much of its equipment and livestock. To support elaborate plans for his colony, he expanded his activities to include Hock Farm on the banks of the Feather River near Yuba City and Sutter's Mill at Coloma. It was at Coloma that he directed James W. Marshall to construct a mill to provide lumber for the needs of his many business interests. With members of the Mormon Battalion, Marshall was close to completion of the mill when he found gold in the mill's tailrace. The discovery of gold and the collapse of his heavily mortgaged business led to financial ruin for Sutter. Prospectors occupied his lands and he was unable to evict them. He left Sutter's Fort and spent a few years at his "Hock Farm" on the Feather River *(See Page 125)* before moving to Lititz, Pennsylvania. He spent the balance of his life here, traveling to Washington, D.C., in vain attempts to petition Congress for restitution for his losses. Sutter, whose development of New Helvetia led to California's gold rush, died without realization of his dreams for his colony here. When Sutter left California, Sutter's Fort fell into disrepair. Now known as Sutter's Fort State Historic Park, it was restored between 1891 and 1893 by the State of California. It became Sutter's Fort State Historic Park in 1947.

Above. School children eat lunch in the shadows of Sutter's Fort State Historic Park.

Below. The Mexican flag depicts the origin of Sutter's Fort.

Opposite Page, Above and Center. Docents bring the history of Sutter's Fort to life for its many visitors.

Opposite Page, Below. The central building within Sutter's Fort is all that remained of the original structure when restoration work began in 1891. In addition to many artifacts from California's gold rush era, displays at Sutter's Fort State Historic Park include tools used by James W. Marshall at Coloma and Kelsey and memorabilia from the Donner Party.

Sacramento

Above. Sacramento, Capitol City of California, is a study in contrasts. Its historic heritage lives on in Old Sacramento, situated on the banks of the Sacramento River with modern skyscrapers serving as a backdrop. Paddle wheelers line the river dock, reminiscent of the gold rush era when they played an important role in transporting miners, equipment and gold up and down the Sacramento River. While Sacramento's origins are in Sutter's Fort, it was not until late 1848 when John Augustus Sutter, Jr. arrived from Switzerland that a plan was drawn up for the town of Sacramento.

Left. The American River, which flows into the Sacramento River at Sacramento, is at flood stage. Unlike gold rush days when Sacramento was frequently flooded, strong levees now protect it from being inundated by spring rains and spring snow melts.

Above. A statue commemorating the Pony Express riders dominates this scene in Old Sacramento. Sacramento was the western terminus of the Pony Express.

Center, Left. The skyline of Old Sacramento includes a number of historic buildings which date to the gold rush era.

Right. The Crocker Art Museum was founded by Edwin B. Crocker, who with his wife Margaret, moved to Sacramento in 1852. They purchased the house in 1868 and had it re-designed for their growing family. Part of the project included the Gallery building which they used to house their collection of art from around the world. Today, the Crocker Art Museum Collection includes sketches and paintings by well known gold rush era artists Charles Christian Nahl, Thomas Hill and Albert Bierstadt.

Sacramento was declared State Capitol of California in 1854. The current Capitol Building, the third structure used by the State of California, was completed in 1874.

Preservation of gold rush era structures in California's gold rush country varies from neglect to success.

Above. This early 20th century structure is the only building that remains at Poker Flat, a rip roaring mining camp in the early 1850's, on the banks of Canyon Creek in Sierra County. Like many such camps, all traces of original gold rush era structures have vanished.

Right. Archeology students from California State University at Sacramento, under the direction of Professor Howard Goldfried, excavate a building site at Virginiatown, near Placerville.

Below, Right. The Wells, Fargo & Company building at Timbuctoo, in Yuba County, was built in 1855. Despite one restoration in 1928, its current owners have tragically refused offers to maintain it and have allowed it to collapse from neglect.

Below, Left. At Columbia, the California Teacher's Association led a penny campaign by students in 1947 to pay for the successful restoration of the Columbia School.

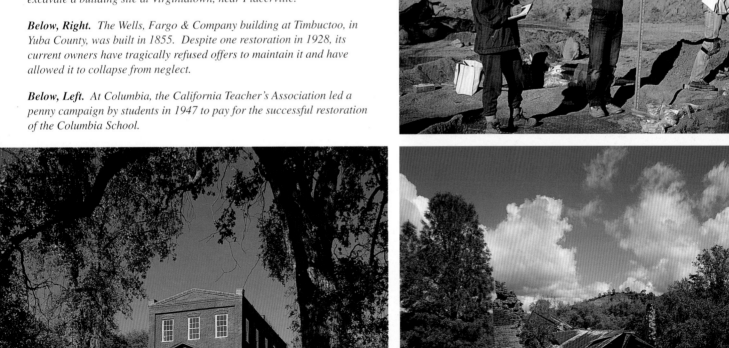

The Northern Mines

From Auburn in the South to Trinity County in the North, the Northern Mines are scattered through the mountainous terrain in some of the most spectacular scenery in the western United States. Forty Niners who mined in Nevada, Sierra, Butte, Plumas, Shasta and Trinity Counties had to cope with steep canyons, fast moving rivers and hillsides covered with poison oak.

The area from Auburn to Nevada City is the most impacted by Twentieth Century development. Of the two dozen traffic signals along the entire length of California Highway 49, all but three are concentrated in this area. Housing tracts have mushroomed along Highway 49. This area has developed into bedroom communities for workers with jobs in Sacramento. Weekend homes for Bay area residents have increased in mountain communities.

Despite all of this development, vast areas of National Forest in Nevada, Sierra, Butte, Plumas, Shasta, and Trinity Counties have minimal roads that allow access into their rugged areas of spectacular beauty. Some of these roads require four wheel drive vehicles but many are easily accessible by passenger cars. Those who explore this region are amply rewarded by vistas rivaled only by a few other areas of North America.

The Northern Mines was the setting for two rushes by men seeking Gold Lake and Gold Bluffs Beach. Both were precipitated by tales of two men who reportedly came upon nuggets the size of their fists. Gold Bluffs Beach did yield a few nuggets but those who participated soon returned south to mine. Although Gold Lake itself was never located, it did open up the gold rich areas on the various branches of the Feather River in Plumas County.

Above. It is in the Northern Mines region that many of the wild, free flowing rivers have been harnessed for recreation, hydroelectricity and water for cities to the south and the west.

Below. Claude Chana was the first white man to discover gold in Auburn Ravine in May 1848. This statue is one of several created by Dr. Kenneth Fox.

Opposite Page. This Pacific Gas and Electric power generating station, Deer Creek Powerhouse, is on the North Fork of the Feather River.

Placer County

Buried beneath the waters of Folsom Lake State
Recreation Area, at the confluence of the North, Middle
and South Forks of the American River, are a number
of important early mining camps. Among these are
Mormon Island, site of discovery of gold by Mormons
who were employed by John A. Sutter to build a flour
mill. Sam Brannan, who started the gold rush in San
Francisco in May 1848, held aloft gold nuggets given to
him by the Mormons who mined here shortly after
Marshall's discovery at nearby Sutter's Mill. Today,
Folsom Lake State Recreation Area is a popular
destination for boaters, fishermen and campers.

Auburn

The diggins at Auburn proved to be some of the richest in all of California's gold rush country, particularly in Auburn Ravine. Important as a gold mining town, Auburn also served as a regional transportation center.

Above. The magnificent Placer County Courthouse at Auburn, the dominant feature of the downtown area, dates from 1894 when it replaced a wooden building built in 1853.

Right. The Chinese who mined the Auburn area are commemorated by this statue in front of the Placer County Chamber of Commerce.

Below. First called Wood's Dry Diggins in 1849, Auburn's Old Town now boasts many gold rush era buildings dating to 1852 including California's oldest post office, left. The three story Auburn Hook and Ladder Company Fire House Number Two, right, was built in 1893 to house the fire company established in 1852.

Above. Visitors to Old Town find a number of shops housed in historic buildings. The buildings on the right are known as the Chinese Merchant's section.

Below. Called Lawyer's Row, these historic buildings now house various antique shops. This building houses the Native Sons of the Golden West on the second floor. It was first built in 1852, burned in 1858 and rebuilt in 1860.

On Church Street in Foresthill, fall foliage mixed with an early snowfall creates a picturesque setting reminiscent of New England.

Foresthill

Foresthill became a trading center in 1850 when miners first began digging on the Foresthill Divide.

Above. *The Old General Store at Foresthill was built in 1859 by the Garrison family.*

Below. *The Foresthill Cemetery overlooks the Foresthill Divide, so called because it separates the Middle Fork of the American River and Shirt Tail Canyon.*

Few areas in California's gold rush country rival the scenic beauty found in the rugged canyons and divides of Shirt Tail Canyon, the Middle Fork of the American River and the Rubicon River. While the rewards were high in this gold rich area, the 49ers experienced great hardships traveling along the divides and into the canyons. Thanks to a network of good roads, today's visitors can travel in relative ease to many of these sites by automobile.

Opposite Page. Huge oak trees grace Big Oak Flat, near Foresthill and above the Middle Fork of the American River. James W. Marshall is reported to have prospected for gold here in 1850.

Above, Right. This modern house at Michigan Bluff sits high above the Middle Fork of the American River. Leland Stanford, founder of Stanford University, reportedly slept on the counter of his store which he operated from 1853 to 1855 at Michigan Bluff.

Below, Right. Deadwood, first mined in 1852 and only seven miles from Michigan Bluff, overlooks the spectacular El Dorado Canyon above the North Fork of the Middle Fork of the American River. All that remains is a small cemetery at the end of a road that is typically passable only by four wheel drive vehicles.

Dutch Flat

Dutch Flat, founded in 1851, is one of the more picturesque of the small mountain towns in the Northern Mines. Its wooden buildings add a quaint charm to this gold rush era town.

Above. The I.O.O.F. building, built in 1858, is still used for local social functions.

Center. The Dutch Flat Hotel, built in 1852, stands empty and fenced off. It is opened periodically for town social functions. The Old Stone Store, built in 1854, stands across the street from the hotel and is still in use.

Below. The Dutch Flat Bakery is one of the numerous well preserved wooden buildings that grace Dutch Flat.

Iowa Hill

Opposite Page, Above. The diggins at Iowa Hill are the most prominent link to the past in this small town where gold was first discovered in 1853.

Opposite Page, Below. The picturesque cemetery at Iowa Hill dates to the gold rush era.

A system of canals beginning high in the Sierras were used to bring water down to the lower elevations for use in hydraulic mining throughout Nevada County.

Opposite Page, Left. *This canal, YB34, a part of the South Yuba Canal system operated by the Nevada (County) Irrigation District in Grass Valley, has its origins at Lake Spaulding.*

Inset. *The historic stone foundation is still intact despite its construction in 1853.*

Washington

Above. *A few buildings remain to denote Washington's gold rush origin in 1849 on the banks of the Yuba River. The rustic Trading Post Cafe, housed in a general store building dating to 1849, is operated by Englishman Colin Haughin in the tradition of times past. The Union Jack is reminiscent of the gold rush days when 49ers flocked from all around the world to the remote canyon camps and towns such as Washington.*

Grass Valley

Named in 1849 for its abundance of green grass, Grass Valley has a well preserved downtown with a number of historic buildings dating to the gold rush era.

Above. The Holbrooke Hotel has welcomed United States' Presidents Ulysses Grant, Benjamin Harrison, Grover Cleveland and James Garfield. Other notable guests include Mark Twain, Bret Harte and Grass Valley celebrity Lotta Crabtree. The Holbrooke Hotel was constructed in 1861 and incorporated the Golden Gate Saloon, built in 1852. The saloon's magnificent bar was shipped by boat around the Horn. It has been in continuous operation since 1851.

Left. Lotta Crabtree, a young protégé of Lola Montez, lived here, just three doors away from Ms. Montez.

Below. Downtown Grass Valley retains much of the charm of its historic past. Pasties, a tasty meat pie dish brought from Cornwall, England, by the Cornish miners who worked deep in the mines of the area, are still popular here. By 1890, Grass Valley was populated heavily by miners and families from Cornwall. A yearly Christmas season feature is the Cornish Christmas Celebration in downtown Grass Valley to commemorate the heritage of its pioneer settlers.

The home of the celebrated dancer, Lola Montez, much renovated since its original construction as a cabin in 1851, now houses the Chamber of Commerce for Grass Valley. Lola created quite a stir in gold rush dance halls with her famous "Spider Dance." Behind her house, right, is the Emanuel Episcopal Church, built in 1858 on land donated by the Gold Hill Mining Company. It is the oldest Episcopal Church in the Northern Mines.

The Bourn Cottage served as home to the manager of the Empire Mine. Both the cottage, and the main mine shaft (Center and Below), are now a part of the Empire Mine State Historic Park.

Quartz (hard-rock) mining had its origins in Grass Valley at the Gold Hill Mine in 1852. Other famous quartz mines in the area include the Eureka and North Star. The Empire Mine combined with the North Star Mine to form one of the largest gold mines in the world. The main shaft extended 4,600 feet on an incline with a lower level that reached to the 8,000 foot level on an incline. When it combined with the North Star, the Empire reached 11,007 feet on an incline or about one vertical mile below the surface. There are more than 367 miles of tunnels. It is estimated that more than $100 million in gold was removed from the Empire Mine during its operation. The North Star Mine, now known as the Nevada County Historical Mining Museum, displays the world's largest Pelton Water Wheel. Built in 1896, it is 30 feet in diameter. The Pelton Water Wheel provided power to operate equipment throughout the Northern Mines. The Pelton Water Wheel's inventor, Lester Allen Pelton, lived and died in nearby Camptonville. (*See page 113*)

Among the many Victorian homes built in Grass Valley in the late 1800's, the Tremoureux House ranks among the loveliest at fall foliage season. This maple, planted here in 1876, was dug up as a sapling from the battlefield at Gettysburg and brought around the Cape Horn.

Nevada City

The largest collection of extant gold rush era buildings in California's gold rush country stands within the historic downtown area of Nevada City. James W. Marshall is reported to have prospected, albeit unsuccessful, in Deer Creek here in mid summer of 1848.

Above, Left. *Firehouse #1, built in 1861, houses the Firehouse Museum.*

Center, Left. *The J. J. Ott Assay Office, right, built in 1863 to replace the original built in 1857, is where the first samples of silver ore from the Washoe Lake area in Nevada were tested. This discovery of the Comstock Lode led to the great silver rush in Nevada City, Nevada in 1859 and heralded the end of the California gold rush. Next door, left, is the Yuba Canal Building, dating from 1855, which served as headquarters to California's largest canal system. Today, it serves as headquarters for the Nevada City Chamber of Commerce.*

Center, Right. *A giant monitor is on display in downtown Nevada City.*

Below. *The Nevada Theatre, dating from 1864, houses the oldest repertory theater in California's gold rush country.*

Above. A modern Bank of America building contrasts
with gold rush era buildings in this winter snow setting.

Center. This Pelton Water Wheel, on display on Main
Street, was used in the nearby Drum Powerhouse on the
Bear River by Pacific Gas & Electric before being
placed on display here in the mid 1980s.

Below. The Kidd-Knox Building was completed in
1856. In the early days of the gold rush, Lola Montez is
reported to have performed her famous "Spider Dance"
in this building. According to Ed Tyson, Nevada County
historian, Lola most likely performed in a dance hall in
the Hamlet-Davis Building which preceded the current
building. On the left is the Masonic Building originally
built in 1864 with an addition completed in 1900.

81

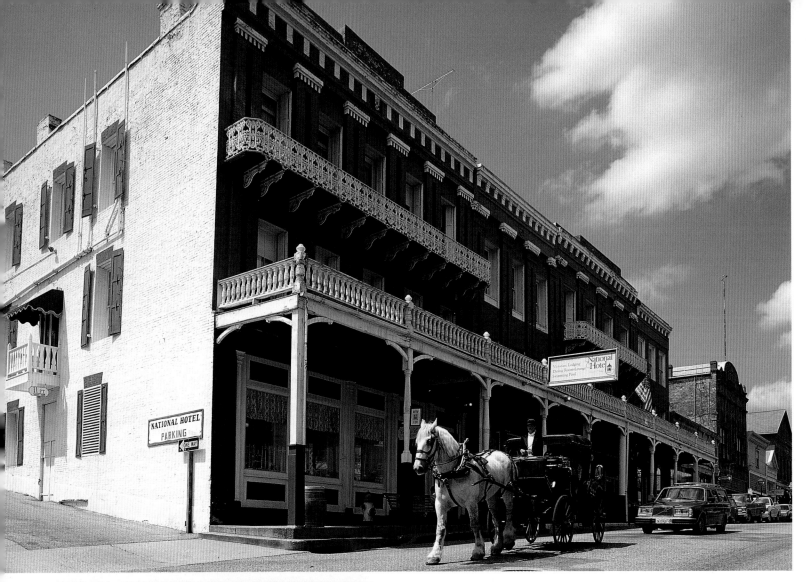

Above. *The National Hotel, completed in 1856, stands as the finest example of gold rush era hotels remaining in California's gold rush country. The National Hotel is the oldest continuously operating hotel in California. Its guests have included Herbert Hoover, Black Bart and Lotta Crabtree. The Pacific Gas and Electric Company was organized here. A horse drawn carriage allows visitors to experience a bygone era.*

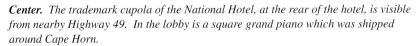

Center. *The trademark cupola of the National Hotel, at the rear of the hotel, is visible from nearby Highway 49. In the lobby is a square grand piano which was shipped around Cape Horn.*

Below, Left. *This building, which now houses the Country Rose Cafe, was built in 1861.*

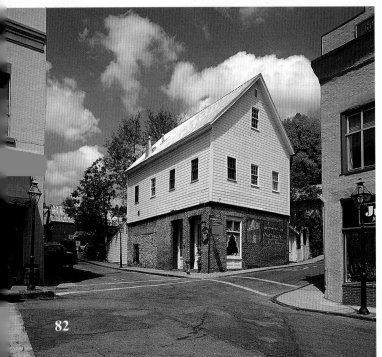

82

Above. The Bridgeport Covered Bridge was constructed over the Middle Fork of the Yuba River in 1862. It is the longest single span covered bridge in the western United States.

Rough And Ready

Below. The I.O.O.F. building, dating to the 1850's, continues to serve as the community hall for Rough and Ready. Rough and Ready is distinguished by its failed effort in early 1850, before California achieved statehood, to form the State of Rough and Ready.

Opposite Page, Below, Right. The Fippin Blacksmith Shop in Rough and Ready is one of a few remaining buildings from the 1850's. It was at the Fippin Blacksmith Shop that Lotta Crabtree danced on the anvil when she was six years old.

No area in California's gold rush country had more hydraulic mining activity than that of northern Nevada County along the San Juan Ridge. This area, on the ancient San Juan River channel, contained, and by many estimates still harbors, hundreds of millions of dollars in gold nuggets. Beginning in the early 1850's, a number of water companies created a series of lakes in the high Sierras in the eastern end of Nevada County and linked them with canals leading along the San Juan Ridge to French Corral at the western end of the county. The intricate system of canals and ditches ran from Bowman Lake down to Graniteville, Malakoff Diggins, North Bloomfield, North San Juan and ended at French Corral. The use of hydraulic mining continued until the 1884 Sawyer Decision when almost all such activity terminated. By this time, most of the creeks and rivers had been clogged with debris washed down from the many diggins and agricultural interests in the valleys below had been harmed.

French Corral

Above. The diggins at French Corral stand as a colorful, silent sentinel to a bygone era. French Corral was the home of the Milton Mining and Water Company and the terminus of the world's first long-distance telephone line. More than sixty miles in length, the long-distance line was built in cooperation with other water companies. It provided communication to help maintain the intricate network of ditches and canals that stretched from French Corral to Bowman Lake.

Below. The sturdy Wells, Fargo & Company building at French Corral, built in 1853, stands beside the highway leading to Bridgeport.

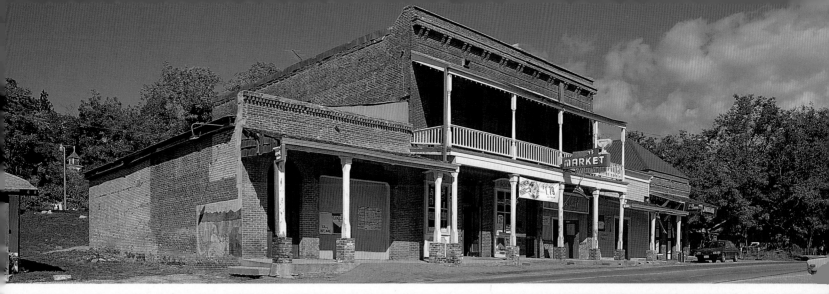

North San Juan

Above. *A few brick buildings are all that remain of historic North San Juan. Set beside Highway 49, these buildings are a sturdy reminder of North San Juan's heyday during the gold rush.*

Below. *Surrounded by the springtime beauty of the golden scotch broom, a young couple fishes in a pond at North San Juan.*

Malakoff Diggins was the largest of the numerous Nevada County diggins. Between 1851 and 1884, when it closed as a result of the Sawyer Decision, approximately $3.5 million of gold were taken from the sluice boxes. Now known as Malakoff Diggins State Historic Park, the site covers more than 3,000 acres, according to Ranger Ken Huie.

Below, Left. The Kings Saloon and the Drug Store at North Bloomfield are reconstructions of earlier historic buildings dating to the 1860's and 1870's.

Below, Right. The E Clampus Vitus are helping to restore the Carter House, used as a hotel when built in 1851.

Below, Left. Numerous wooden dams were built in the high Sierra to supply water for hydraulic mining. The water to operate the monitors (See ii) at Malakoff Diggins came from Bowman Lake through the North Bloomfield ditch operated by the North Bloomfield Gravel Mining Company. This historic picture shows the original Bowman Lake Dam.

Below, Right. More than 150 years later, the Malakoff Diggins serve as a stark reminder of the efforts made by miners to dig away hillsides in their frantic search for gold.

Sierra County

Downieville

Settled in 1851, Downieville is among the prettiest towns in California's gold rush country, nestled in a forested canyon at the confluence of the Downie River and the North Fork of the Yuba River. Named for William Downie who came here in November 1849 to prospect, the area quickly proved to be rich in gold. Downieville was spared the devastating fires that destroyed entire districts of early gold rush towns. For this reason, and with five buildings dating from 1852, its downtown area appears much as it did during the gold rush days. Sierra County presented a number of challenges to the 49ers. Because of steep canyon walls surrounding many of its rivers, access was difficult for the 49ers.

Today's visitors find a number of paved roads providing access to the remote areas. Sierra County's rugged beauty is well worth the visit.

Above. Built in 1852, the Craycroft Building served first as the Craycroft Saloon. The saloon's 70 foot bar was the longest ever in California's gold rush country. Juanita, a Mexican woman who stabbed to death a miner who attacked her, fled here for protection in 1852. Despite her protests that she acted only in self defense, Juanita became the only woman to be hung in California's gold rush country.

89

The Mountain Messenger

Above, Left. *Downieville's rugged setting is readily illustrated in this spring scene. The white church steeple, above the bridge over the Yuba River, belongs to the Methodist Church. Built in 1852, it is the oldest Protestant church in continuous use in California.*

Above, Right. *The Mountain Messenger, housed in an 1852 stone building, is California's oldest weekly newspaper. It was established in 1853.*

Below. *The Hirschfelder Building, also built in 1852, now serves as a grocery store. The Bell Tower, on the right, was erected in 1896 and used to sound the fire alarm.*

Opposite Page, Above. *The Immaculate Conception Church was built in 1858.*

Sierra City
Opposite Page, Below. *Situated below the majestic Sierra Buttes, the Busch Building was built in 1871 in Sierra City. The Busch Building later served as the Wells, Fargo & Company office. The second largest gold nugget discovered in California's gold rush country, weighing about 133 pounds, was taken from the Monumental Quartz Mine in the Sierra Buttes.*

91

Opposite Page, Above. The Kentucky Mine Museum, operated by Sierra County, one mile east of Sierra City, has excellent displays which depict the operation of a 10-stamp quartz mill. The setting, just below the 8,587 feet high Sierra Buttes, is scenic in all seasons.

Opposite Page, Below, Left. In the remote northwest corner of Sierra County, these ruins of the Port Wine Store, dating from the 1850s and a small cemetery nearby, set among remnants of dry diggins, are all that remain to be seen at Port Wine. This rugged area, which includes the sites of the 1850s mining towns of Queen City, Gibsonville, Howland Flat and Poker Flat, provides visitors with spectacular views.

Opposite Page, Below, Right. At Goodyear's Bar, on Highway 49 and at the confluence of Goodyear's Creek and the North Fork of the Yuba River, the venerable St. Charles Hotel, built in 1864, was a stagecoach stop on the Alleghany to Downieville Road. Today it serves as a very comfortable Bed & Breakfast Inn. Bullet holes decorate the ceiling of the dining room and its walls tilt because someone forgot to shovel the snow from the roof many years ago.

Above. This scenic setting on the North Fork of the Yuba River near Downieville is adjacent to Highway 49.

Center. Only a few houses, an old church and an I.O.O.F. Hall remain at Forest to recall its importance as a gold mining camp in the early 1850s.

Below. The Original 16-1 Mine at Alleghany, on the scenic Pliocene Ridge that runs between the Middle and North Forks of the Yuba River, was discovered in 1896. It has been worked over the years with varying degrees of success. However, in 1995, a rich strike was made and prospects are good for this mine to produce well into the future.

The majestic Sierra Buttes reflect serenely in Sand Pond near Bassett's Station. The Sierra Buttes are a major landmark in the area and can be seen for many miles. While Sand Pond is man made from the excavation of tailings from the nearby Young America Mine, this area is rich in natural lakes.

This Gold Lake, the largest and northernmost of the Sierra County lake region, is the namesake of the fabled "Gold Lake" that resulted in a rush of epic proportions because of one 49er named Stoddard. In the fall of 1849, Stoddard was in an emigrant party traveling along the Lassen Trail in northern Plumas County when he became lost. Along the way, he reportedly stumbled upon a lake filled with gold nuggets somewhere between Downieville and Sierra Valley (in Plumas County). When he reached safety along the North Fork of the Yuba River and related his story to other miners, it was too late in the season to go back up into the mountains at that time. In the spring of 1850, however, he was joined by several thousand anxious miners who followed him through the lakes to the area of the Middle Fork of the Feather River in Plumas County. While Stoddard was unable to find his fabled "Gold Lake," his tale is credited with opening up this region to successful mining in the gold rich rivers of Plumas County.

Opposite Page, Above. Golden trout are plentiful in Gold Lake as this colorful specimen attests.

Below, Left and Right. Early morning is the best time for fishermen to head out to their favorite fishing spot.

Above, Left. *A solitary fisherman hopes for a strike from a trout in the Yuba River.*

Above, Right. *Pacific dogwoods turns hills and mountains white in the spring.*

Below. *Sardine Lake, at sunset, reflects the beauty of the Sierra Lakes Region.*

Opposite Page, Above. *A number of trails were opened to stagecoach roads through the region connecting Marysville with La Porte, La Porte with Quincy and Johnsville. Each of these roads today provides spectacular vistas just as beautiful as when the 49ers passed here during the gold rush era. A number of the mountain peaks in the area soar above the 7,000 foot mark. This setting was photographed on the La Porte - Quincy road near Pilot Peak.*

Opposite Page, Below. *The Union Hotel, circa 1855, still serves excellent meals and provides lodging to guests at La Porte in Plumas County. Thanks to the fabled "Gold Lake" rush of 1850, Plumas County — also a mountainous region with steep canyon walls down to its creeks and rivers — was opened to the 49ers who found numerous rich gold deposits. The area around La Porte bears stark evidence of hydraulic mining activity.*

The road to Poker Flat requires four wheel drive to negotiate the steep descent into the Canyon Creek Canyon.

Onion Valley, on the La Porte — Quincy Road near Pilot Peak, was found to be rich in gold deposits in July 1850. The valley is named for the abundance of wild onions which bloom here in the summer.

Fall is an especially attractive season along the La Porte — Quincy Road.

Deep canyons and 7,000 foot plus peaks add to the beauty of this area along the La Porte — Johnsville Road.

Plumas - Eureka State Park

The northernmost and highest in elevation, The Plumas - Eureka State Park is also in the most scenic setting of the state parks in California's gold rush country. In the shadow of 7,490 foot Eureka Peak, a number of mining operations commenced in 1851.

By 1943, when the stamp mills fell silent, more than $25 million in gold had been removed from the 65 miles of tunnels in Eureka Peak.

Today, through an extensive preservation program that began in 1959, Plumas - Eureka State Park is a shining gem in the California State Park System.

Above and Opposite Page, Center. With the centerpiece, the Plumas - Eureka Mine, as a back drop, an old bunkhouse serves as an excellent museum and numerous buildings and equipment provide interpretative displays that allow a glimpse into the gold rush era.

Opposite Page, Below. Colorful snow plants (Sarcodes sanguinea) are found in the campgrounds and wooded areas of the park.

Center. These handmade snow skis were used by the legendary John "Snowshoe" Thompson, a native of Norway. From January 1856, Thompson made frequent winter mail runs across the Sierra Nevada at Carson Pass for twenty years. In nearby Johnsville, a plaque notes that the area was the site of winter sports competitions beginning in 1860.

Below, Left. Hands on is the rule at a number of exhibits for children who visit the museum.

Below, Right. Johnsville, an interesting old mining town dating to 1872, is privately owned. The Johnsville Hotel was built in 1908.

Quincy

The scenic American Valley was first settled in 1852. One of the three founders of Plumas County selected his American Ranch as the site for Quincy, named after his hometown in Illinois.

Opposite Page, Above. Horses graze in this bucolic setting with 7,017 foot Spanish Peak in the distance. Spanish Peak, Spanish Creek and Spanish Ranch were named for two Mexicans who settled there in 1850. The famed Monte Cristo Mine tunneled into Spanish Peak.

Opposite Page, Below. Dairy cattle graze in the American Valley. The valley is surrounded by forested mountains which provide a major source of income for the area. Most of Plumas County is within the Plumas National Forest.

Above. Nelson's Point, at the confluence of Nelson Creek with the Middle Fork of the Feather River, was mined out by members of the "Gold Lake" rush in 1850.

Below. One of the best displays in California's gold rush country recounts local history at the Plumas County Museum in Quincy. Displays include those of Indian heritage, early pioneers and Chinese miners.

RICH BAR

GOLD FIRST FOUND HERE JULY 1850 BY MINERS COMING
OVER MOUNTAINS FROM THE YUBA DIGGINS.
MUCH PRODUCTION DURING EARLY FIFTIES ALONG THIS
EAST BRANCH OF THE FEATHER RIVER'S NORTH FORK.
HERE "DAME SHIRLEY" (LOUISE AMELIA KNAPP
SMITH CLAPPE) WROTE HER LETTERS FROM THE
CALIFORNIA MINES, ONE OF THE FOREMOST CLASSICS
OF THE GOLD RUSH.

REGISTERED HISTORICAL LANDMARK NO. 337

PLAQUE PLACED BY CALIFORNIA STATE PARK COMMISSION
IN COOPERATION WITH LAS PLUMAS DE ORO CHAPTER
OF E CLAMPUS VITUS, SEPTEMBER 13, 1957.

Rich Bar

Rich Bar was discovered by members of the "Gold Lake" rush in July of 1850. Rich Bar proved to be the richest river bar in California's gold rush country. It is estimated that $4 million in gold was removed from Rich Bar. It was common for miners to find hundreds of ounces of gold in a single day. While this small bar on the East Branch of the North Fork of the Feather River was rich in gold, one of its residents, Louise Amelia Knapp Smith Clappe (better known as Dame Shirley), provided scholars with a rich and detailed account of daily life in a river bar camp. From her arrival in September 1851 with her husband, Fayette Clappe, a Doctor, until her departure in late 1852, she wrote exquisite detail about every facet of life — and death — at Rich Bar.

PAN FOR GOLD
RICH BAR MINING CO

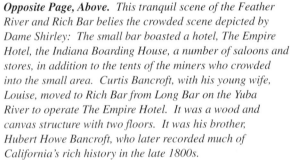

Opposite Page, Above. This tranquil scene of the Feather River and Rich Bar belies the crowded scene depicted by Dame Shirley: The small bar boasted a hotel, The Empire Hotel, the Indiana Boarding House, a number of saloons and stores, in addition to the tents of the miners who crowded into the small area. Curtis Bancroft, with his young wife, Louise, moved to Rich Bar from Long Bar on the Yuba River to operate The Empire Hotel. It was a wood and canvas structure with two floors. It was his brother, Hubert Howe Bancroft, who later recorded much of California's rich history in the late 1800s.

Opposite Page, Center, Left. Rich Bar of today is owned by Norman Grant. According to Grant, who operates the Rich Bar Mining Company, there is still much gold to be discovered here.

Opposite Page, Below, Left. A prospector "crevices" in solid rock trying to find elusive nuggets.

Opposite Page, Below, Right. Prospectors carry buckets of dirt to the sluicing station to pan out for nuggets.

Above, Left. Erin Kelly tries her luck at panning.

Above, Right. Veteran prospectors discuss the techniques of panning.

Below. A veteran miner spills water as he moves the pan back and forth, seeking the glint of gold in the bottom.

Center. This is what it is all about, gold from Rich Bar!

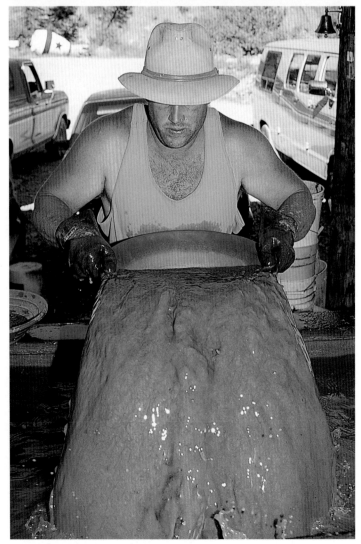

The twenty three letters from "Dame Shirley" to her sister Molly in Massachusetts, written in 1851 and 1852, were published by *The Pioneer*, a San Francisco monthly magazine, in 1854 and 1855. Historians have been able to compare her lengthy manuscripts with diaries of others who visited Rich Bar during her time there to cross reference events. One of the best known, which corraborates many of the incidents at Rich Bar, is that of Adolphus Windeler *"The California Gold Rush Diary of a German Sailor"*, edited by W. Turrentine Jackson. Indeed, Californian historians Josiah Royce and Hubert H. Bancroft acknowledged the importance of her letters. Bret Harte even used Dame Shirley's descriptions of incidents at Rich Bar as the basis for his *The Outcasts of Poker Flat* and *The Luck of Roaring Camp*.

Left. Soon after Dame Shirley arrived at Rich Bar in 1851, Nancy Anne Bailey, one of the two other women in the camp died. Her grave marker stands in the small cemetery above the river bar where she died on September 30, 1851.

Below, Left. *Accidents in the gold mines and along the rivers of California's gold rush country often led to disastrous results for those involved. Today, with expert assistance from search and rescue units, help is usually available and often within an hour or less thanks to the various county service units. Here, a fisherman, unable to get back up the slope to the railway, waits patiently for help. Led by Lt. Mike Grant of the Plumas County Sheriff's Department, members of the rescue squad quickly pulled him to safety.*

The Sierra Valley at the eastern edge of Plumas County held the key to early development and opening of this area to agriculture. On the east side of the valley, James P. Beckwourth discovered the lowest pass in the Sierra Nevada. Now called Beckwourth Pass, it is just 5,221 feet high. More importantly, it is composed of generally flat soil and virtually rock free. The Pass marks the beginning of the Beckwourth Trail which leads to Marysville in Yuba County. Citizens of Marysville hired Beckwourth to build it to lure pioneers to their town.

Above. This farm in the Sierra Valley, at Vinton, is near the site of the Beckwourth Trail.

Center, Left and Right. The Oregon - California Trail Association, based in Independence, Missouri, helps to preserve and to mark the historic trails used by emigrants and 49ers. Here, Ford Osborn (left to right), Andy Hammond, Warren Gibson and Kevin McCormick, verify the location of a newly placed marker on the Beckwourth Trail in Grizzly Valley, just west of Sierra Valley.

Below, Left. California Highway 49 ends here at Vinton.

Yuba County

Above. *The Oregon Creek Covered Bridge, at the eastern edge of Yuba County, just off Highway 49, was built in 1862.*

Opposite Page, Above. *At Camptonville, this monument memorializes Lester Allen Pelton's invention of the Pelton Water Wheel and its important role in gold mining in the Northern Mines.*

Opposite Page, Below. *The Country Store at Dobbin's Ranch dates to 1867. There is an old theatre, used to entertain locals, in the store.*

113

Above. The P & L Mercantile at Brown's Valley on the Marysville - La Porte Road occupies a stone store built in 1849. Across the road, ruins of a hotel — one of five built during the 1850s — dating to 1852 can still be seen among the blackberry vines.

Below. The Rackerby Stage Stop, built in 1861 on the Marysville - La Porte Road, is quite colorful in the spring.

Above. The lovely Woodleaf Hotel, built as the Woodville House in 1856, was a California Stage Company station on the Marysville - La Porte Road.

Below. These ruins are the only visible reminders of the once bustling Frenchtown.

Above. Only the depression of the basement remains at the site of the Empire Ranch Station, part of the California Stage Company, at Smartville. Kimberly Silva of nearby Smartville stops to smell a rose possibly planted during the gold rush era.

Below. At Smartville, this canal maintained by the Nevada Irrigation District serves as a source of water for cattle. The Smartville Cemetery can be seen on the distant hill in this bucolic scene. Just down the road is Timbuctoo, where the Wells, Fargo & Company building dating to 1855 is in ruins. (See Page 61) Both Smartville and Timbuctoo were the sites of significant hydraulic mining activity. Much of the debris that raised the Yuba River by 70 feet at Marysville and required the building of levees to protect the town from flooding came from this area. The remnants of Sucker Flat are just north of Smartville.

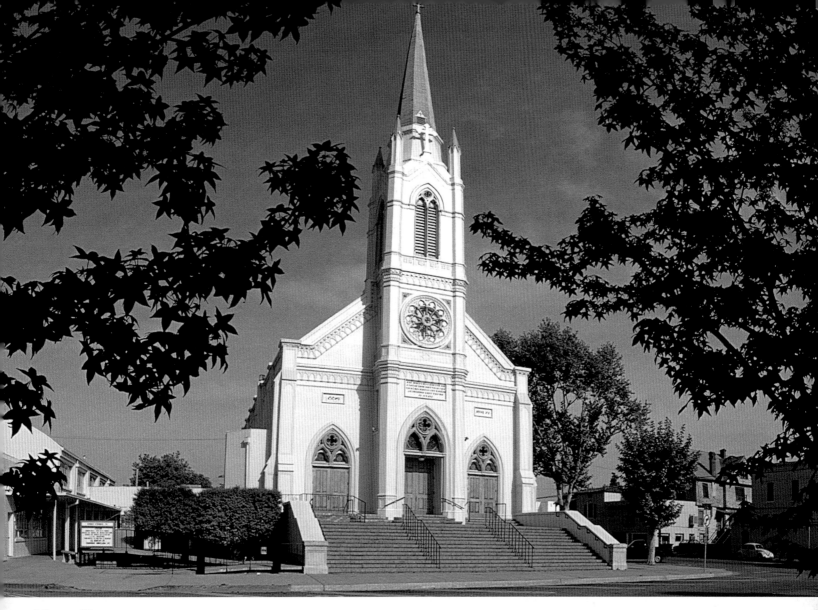

Marysville

Marysville was built on land that was originally part of John Sutter's Ranch. On January 18, 1850, city officials were elected, making the Town of Marysville older than the State of California. Charles Covillaud, one of the founders, had Marysville named for his wife, Mary Murphy Covillaud, a survivor of the Donner Party tragedy. During the early days of the California gold rush, the Feather River was navigable to Marysville. Marysville prospered as a result of its proximity

to the Northern Mines. Miners traveled upriver from San Francisco to Marysville before taking one of the numerous trails leading to the many gold mining camps. Despite the destructive floods which resulted from debris from upriver hydraulic mining choking the Yuba River, a number of historic buildings from the gold rush era at Marysville remain. Marysville was the site of the first Macy's Store in California. In 1850, Rowland H. Macy left Boston — where he had been unsuccessful in several ventures — to try his luck at retailing in Marysville. He had no better luck in Marysville. He returned east and opened a small, fancy dry goods store in New York City in 1858. Today, Macy's is one of the world's largest retailers.

Page 117, Above. The magnificent neo-gothic structure, St. Joseph's Catholic Church, was built in 1855.

Page 117, Below. The building housing the Mary Aaron Museum, with excellent displays of local history, was completed in 1856.

Above, Left. When the Bok Kai Temple was first built in the 1850s, it looked down on the Yuba River. Because sediment from hydraulic mining raised the level of the river, the temple is now behind a levee and below river level. The current building was constructed in 1880. The Silver Dollar Saloon, built in 1860, has served as a bar and a hotel. It also served as a brothel until 1975.

Opposite Page, Lower, Left. The entrance to the Bok Kai Temple faces the levee along the Yuba River.

Lower, Right. The altar in the temple is covered with many prayer offerings.

In 1844, William Johnson purchased land owned by Pablo Gutierrez, an employee of John Sutter, on the north side of the Yuba River. Johnson, first husband of Mary Murphy of the Donner Party, settled here and built an adobe house which became well known as Johnson's Rancho to thousands of emigrants who followed the Bear River route down the Sierra Nevada to Sacramento. Numerous diaries recount the hospitality accorded by Johnson to emigrants who were in need of help. It was to Johnson's Rancho that the seven members of the Forlorn Hope Party stumbled on January 7, 1847. The remaining members of the ill-fated Donner Party — including Mary Murphy — were brought here when finally rescued in February 1847.

Rediscovered in 1985 by Jack Steed, author of The Donner Party Rescue Site, walls of Johnson's Rancho can be seen as a gentle rise in the grass across the center of the foreground and a line along the right side of the scene. Early Twentieth Century dredging for gold in the adjacent Bear River stopped just a few yards short of destroying the site.

Inset. *Jack Steed displays a number of artifacts discovered at the site to history buffs.*

Above. *According to Jack Steed, this spot was the end of the way west at Johnson's Rancho, on the banks of the Bear River, for some emigrants who made the trek on the California Trail. While most continued on to Sutter's Fort at Sacramento to the south, others turned north to the Feather River or Shasta and Weaverville.*

Left, Center. *Here, riders in period costumes recreate pioneer travel along the trail from Rough and Ready to Wheatland by way of Johnson's Rancho. The annual event commemorates the trail's importance in the early development of California.*

Left, Below. *Sunrise at Johnson's Rancho, with the Sierra Nevada in the distance, colors early morning clouds.*

Opposite Page, Above. *Almonds are one of the important agricultural crops in this region. This almond grove near Yuba City presents a lovely spring setting.*

Opposite Page, Below. *At Long's Bar, on the Yuba River, huge mounds of rocks dredged from the river in the early 1900s are piled almost a hundred feet high on the river bank. The distant Sutter Buttes in adjacent Sutter County are clearly visible.*

Sutter County

Above. *Visible from many miles in all directions, the Sutter Buttes were named for John Augustus Sutter. Almond trees and yellow mustard flowers create a colorful setting at sunrise near Yuba City.*

Below, Left. *White and pink almond blossoms in the orchard of Jimmie Lachman at Sutter, California, frame the Sutter Buttes.*

Opposite Page, Below, Right. *Remnants of Sutter's Hock Farm south of Yuba City were used to create this memorial to his early agricultural efforts.*

Opposite Page, Above. *The I.O.O.F. building at Forbestown was built in 1855.*

Opposite Page, Below. *The Mountain House, on the Beckwourth Trail, is the second structure on this site. The grapevine is from the original house and dates to the late 1850's.*

Oroville

Oroville, which means "City of Gold," is one of the loveliest cities in the Northern Mines. In the spring, flowers color the gardens of Oroville, the valley and on Table Mountain above this town which was first called Ophir City. In 1854 and 1855, there were some 10,000 miners in and around Oroville, making it the largest city in California's gold rush country at the time.

Above. *The C. F. Lott House, built in 1856, is a Victorian gothic revival style house located in Oroville. The Lott House's formal garden, one of only two dating to the gold rush era that remain in California's gold rush country, forms the setting for the lovely Sank Park.*

Below. *The Chinese Temple, built in 1863, was the religious center of Oroville's large community of Chinese. The temple's three chapels, various exhibits and Chinese gardens, provide an excellent view into this important aspect of the Chinese miner's life during California's gold rush era.*

Bidwell Bar, named after John Bidwell who came west with the Bidwell - Bartleson Party in 1841, now lies below the waters of Lake Oroville. Bidwell found gold here in 1848 on the Middle Fork of the Feather River. Bidwell Bar was the Butte County seat from 1853 to 1856, until the county seat was moved to Oroville.

Above. This suspension bridge, manufactured on the east coast of the United States and shipped by boat around Cape Horn, was installed across the Middle Fork of the Feather River in 1856 at Bidwell Bar. The bridge was in use until 1954 when it was closed to vehicles. When the Oroville Lake project was created, the bridge was moved to its current location at Bidwell Canyon in 1968.

Below. John Bidwell built his mansion in what is now Chico. Attaining the rank of General in the California Militia, Bidwell was prominent in state politics and agriculture. His house and grounds are now maintained as the Bidwell Mansion State Historic Park.

Opposite Page. A crescent moon rides high in the sky above a flock of vultures taking to the air above Lake Oroville just before dawn. Oroville Dam, completed in 1968, is the tallest (770 feet) and largest earth dam in the United States. Oroville Lake, a project of the State Department of Water Resources, covers more than 24 square miles. The lake covers the largest gold dredger tailings in California's gold rush country.

Above Oroville, and visible for many miles, Table Mountain is one of the interesting geological features of the area. In the spring and summer it is covered with many flowers of various types. Here, with a snow storm in the background, cattle graze peacefully in sunshine amidst scenic grandeur.

Cherokee

Years of hydraulic mining created the world's largest diggins where millions of dollars in gold were unearthed by the Spring Valley Hydraulic Gold Company and its predecessors. In addition, this was the site of the first discovery of diamonds in California. Discovered by white settlers in 1849, and named for a band of Cherokee Indians from Oklahoma who mined here, the town of Cherokee was founded in 1853. The Cherokee diggins were so rich that claims were limited to 100 feet square. By 1876, all of the mining operations in the area merged into the Spring Valley Hydraulic Gold Company, with over 100 miles of tunnels and flumes to bring water to operate 18 monitors, it became the world's largest hydraulic gold mine. Cherokee boasted seventeen saloons, eight hotels, two schools, three churches, several lodges, a race track and a brewery. To celebrate America's centennial, the world's largest gold bar was cast at Cherokee. It weighed in at 260 pounds avoirdupois or 317 pounds troy and was valued at $76,000. Four years later, in 1880, Cherokee was visited by President Rutherford B. Hayes and wife, Lucy, General W. T. Sherman and General John Bidwell. A year later, however, as with most towns in California's gold rush country, a disastrous fire destroyed much of Cherokee.

Above. Sugar Loaf Mountain rises above the site of the Spring Valley Mine at Cherokee on the north side of Table Mountain.

Below. The Cherokee Mine Superintendent's house now serves as the Cherokee Museum. According to Curator Jim Lenhoff, of Oroville, the Cherokee Museum has served in prior years as a stage stop, a residence and miners' boarding house.

Opposite Page, Above. The remains of the Spring Valley Mine and Assay Office, burned in a fire in 1947, are near the Cherokee Museum.

Opposite Page, Below. The Oregon City School, built in 1877, is the only remnant of the once thriving Oregon City. It now houses a museum. Oregon City was founded in 1848 with the arrival here of a group of Oregonians. The group was led by Peter Burnett who became the first civil Governor of California.

Shasta County

Shasta State Historic Park

First settled in 1849 as Reading's Springs, it was renamed in 1850 as Shasta. During its glory days of the early 1850s, Shasta was a large gold mining camp and also a major business and transportation hub for northern California.

Above. A colorful rainbow shines above the Masonic Lodge at Shasta State Historic Park. The building was constructed in 1854 by Julius North and Silas Tucker to house a mercantile business. The Masonic Lodge acquired the third floor that same year and the entire building in 1859. The charter for Western Star Number Two was brought from Missouri by Peter Lassen (of Lassen Trail fame) in 1848.

Below. The large Bull, Baker and Company building was built in 1853. One partner bought goods in San Francisco and shipped them up the Sacramento River to Red Bluff. A second partner transported the goods on wagons to Shasta City where the third partner sold them to the 49ers.

Inset. While much of historic Shasta lies in ruins, well marked remnants of the gold mining era provide a glimpse of its past. Courtesy of Shasta State Historic Park

Opposite Page, Above. The Catholic Church at French Gulch was built in 1905. Several gold rush era hotels are nearby.

Opposite Page, Below. A deer pauses to pose for the photographer at Lewiston.

135

Weaverville

Weaverville was established on July 8, 1850, when its first three inhabitants, John Weaver, John Howe and Daniel Bennett, built a cabin. They drew pine needles to pick the name with Weaver pulling out the winning needle. Weaverville was isolated from the gold rush towns of the Sierra Nevada because of its location in the rugged Trinity Mountains. Until 1858 when a wagon road was built from Shasta, only pack trails were available to haul goods in and gold out of Weaverville. Downtown Weaverville appears much as it did during the gold rush era and is listed on the National Register of Historic Places. A number of buildings are still in use that date to the early 1850's.

Above. The county courthouse, left, built in 1856, served as a hotel and saloon. A number of historic buildings have circular iron staircases leading to second floor balconies. Each floor had separate owners which necessitated the building of outside staircases for access. The Weaverville Drugstore, right, currently owned and operated by Frank Hicks, Jr., and Patricia Hicks, has been in business since 1852. The Weaverville Drugstore is the oldest continuously operating drugstore in California's gold rush

country. *The town of Weaverville is considered one of the most scenic settings in California's gold rush country.*

Opposite Page, Below. *The Trinity County Courthouse building, purchased in 1865, is the second oldest courthouse in California's gold rush country.*

Below, Right. *The Einfalt and Hoslinger building, built in the summer of 1856, still stands proudly with its circular stairway to the second level. On the right is the 1856 Tinnin Building. This building is an excellent example of the various fireproof buildings dating from the 1850's. The historic Trinity Journal, published weekly since January 26, 1856, has occupied the building since 1989. Courtesy of Patricia Johnsen Hicks, author of* **Weaverville.**

137

Opposite Page, Above. *The Brewery Restaurant is housed in the old Pacific Brewery Building built by Fred Walters in 1855.*

Opposite Page, Below. *One of the more interesting of the remaining Chinese temples in California's gold rush county, called the WON LIM MIAO ("Temple Amongst the Forest Beneath the Clouds"), is at Weaverville. The temple is now preserved as the Weaverville Joss House State Historic Park. This building, built to replace an 1852 or 1853 temple at Chimney Point that burned in 1873, was completed in 1874. The temple houses a number of artifacts important to its Chinese heritage. Particularly of interest are artifacts from the 1854 Tong War.*

Above. *Just west of Weaverville is the site of the La Grange Mine. During its operations, it was one of the three largest hydraulic mining operations in California's gold rush country. This monitor was one of many used to wash away most of the mountainside in the background.*

Below. *Huge piles of rocks at Junction City on the Trinity River mark the remains of the most western dredging in California's gold rush country.*

Above. Only this building, which dates to 1859, marks the site of Helena.

Opposite Page. Kayakers paddle the Trinity River in a heavy downpour near Cedar Flat.

Below. French Bar on the Trinity River was heavily mined in the early 1850's. The scars of mining activity, dating to recent years, are visible.

Humboldt County

Reminiscent of the rush to the fabled Gold Lake in Sierra County, some 5,000 miners flocked to Gold Bluffs Beach on the Pacific Ocean in Humboldt County when a miner reported golden nuggets the size of his fist scattered over the beach. Small nuggets were found but nothing near the size reported by the unidentified 49er. Today, visitors find a beautiful, sandy beach with golden bluffs. Of interest, too, is a herd of elk that roams the beach and bluff area.

Gold Bluffs Beach is a part of the Prairie Creek Redwood State Park near Orick.

Southern Mines

The Southern Mines range from Auburn to Mariposa County in the south. The majority of this area is along California's Highway 49 and is readily accessible to visitors. While the Northern Mines can boast of rugged mountain scapes, the Southern Mines have, flower for flower, the most colorful hills in all of California's gold rush country.

Snow and cold weather did not impact the 49ers who mined the Southern Mines as severely as it did the miners working the Northern Mines. But during the winter, rain and the snow melt from the higher elevations flooded the rivers in both areas.

While the peaks of the mountains of the Northern Mines are rock covered, those of the Southern Mines are usually pine shrouded gentle slopes. In late afternoon the sun shining through the trees creates pleasing vistas of light and shadow.

El Dorado County's county seat is at Placerville. Now a peaceful town among apple orchards and vineyards, it was known in the gold rush days as Hangtown Amador County comes alive in the spring with flowers throughout its wine country. Calaveras County is widely known as the setting for "The Celebrated Jumping Frog of Calaveras County," written by Mark Twain. Tuolumne County is a major locale for western themed movies. Mariposa County is distinguished as being the gateway to Yosemite Valley. Yosemite National Park first became a tourist attraction in the mid 1850s soon after its discovery by Major Savage of the Mariposa Battalion.

The El Dorado County Chamber of Commerce building, covered with ivy, is quite colorful in the Fall.

Placerville

Placerville has been known by several names since its founding in 1848. It was first called Old Dry Diggins. After its citizens took law and order into their own hands and hung three men in 1849, it became known as Hangtown. Finally, in May 1854, it was incorporated as Placerville. The entire region around Placerville was rich in gold. Indeed, Coloma is just eight miles from Placerville. Hangtown Creek, which runs through downtown Placerville, yielded large quantities of gold. In addition to its role as a gold mining town, Placerville was an important distribution point for towns and camp to the north and south. John Mohler Studebaker came to Placerville in 1853. He spent the next five years earning his gold, as did many other merchants, by selling his wares. A blacksmith, he produced and sold wheelbarrows, shovels, picks and other tools. He took his fortune earned in California's gold rush country, invested it with brothers Henry and Clement and helped build the Studebaker Company into a major vehicle manufacturing concern (first wagons, then cars and trucks). Placerville became the county seat in 1857 when it was moved from Coloma.

Above. Downtown Placerville still retains a number of historic buildings dating to the gold rush era.

Opposite Page, Above. This view of Hangtown (now Placerville) was taken in the early 1850's.

Opposite Page, Below. Miners used this sluice box to mine for gold. Chinese workers, right, and Americans work side by side.

El Dorado County

Above. This ruin, dating to 1859, is the only readily visible gold rush era landmark at Gold Hill.

Left. California's gold rush country has many old barns and garages, some with antique pickup trucks. At Gold Hill, this spring setting seems contradictory with a Dodge parked in a garage that is labeled with a Ford sign.

Opposite Page, Above. El Dorado County is well known today for its excellent wines and apple orchards. The local agricultural heritage is celebrated each fall with Apple Days at Placerville.

Opposite Page, Below. At Diamond Springs, the I.O.O.F. building, dating to 1859, is still used for local social activities.

Above. *Georgetown, first established in 1849, was known then as Growlersburg. After fire destroyed Growlersburg in 1852, the town was rebuilt as Georgetown. That fire was much like those which destroyed many other towns and camps in California's gold rush country. However, to reduce the chance of another fire destroying the entire town, Georgetown's main street was built one hundred feet wide. The Georgetown Hotel, right, was built in 1896.*

Center, Right. *This section of buildings on Main Street dates to July 1856.*

Center, Left. *The I.O.O.F. Hall was built in 1859 as the Balsar House. The hall is still used for local social activities.*

Below. *The Wells, Fargo & Company building, now a popular cafe, was constructed in 1852.*

Georgetown

Georgetown is known as the "Pride of the Mountains." The clear air, beautiful mountain setting and stately trees make it a favorite tourist destination. In the fall, it is especially pretty when the trees are colored brightly.

Above. *The American River Inn, dating to 1899, replaced the original American Hotel (circa 1853) that burned in the same year.*

Below. *Many fruit trees have thrived around Georgetown since their planting in the gold rush era.*

Opposite Page, Above. The Bayley House stands beside Highway 49 at Pilot Hill. The house was built in 1862 when Alcandor A. Bayley believed that the railroad would pass nearby.

Opposite Page, Center. Sunrise through fog accentuates the beauty of these huge oaks near Coloma. They were witness to the passing of the 49ers.

Opposite Page, Below, Left. The Sierra Nevada House, at Lotus, dates to 1850. Lotus, near Coloma, was first named Marshall in honor of James W. Marshall.

Opposite Page, Below, Right. The Coloma Country Inn, built in 1852, is one of a number of historic private buildings at Coloma that date to gold rush days. Innkeepers Cindi and Allan Ehrgott operate it as a comfortable Bed and Breakfast Inn, keeping with its historic heritage.

Above. This gold rush era building is the only remnant of the once thriving town of Newtown at the northern end of Pleasant Valley.

Center, Left. Wild turkeys forage in this field near Highway 49.

Center, Right. Only a few tombstones remain to remind visitors to Grizzly Flats of its rich heritage.

Below. El Dorado County is lovely in the fall as depicted in this scenic setting near Mt. Aukom.

151

Amador County

Amador County was found to be rich in gold during the gold rush era. Today, it is a major destination for many tourists who visit California's gold rush country. The Shenandoah Valley, east of Plymouth, produces some of the best wines in California.

Above. Sobon Estate Vineyards now occupy the historic D'Agostini lands which were established in 1856.

Below, Left. The original stone cellar and several of the vats from the D'Agostini Winery are still used by Sobon Estate Vineyards.

Below, Right. A visitor to Sobon Estate Vineyards tastes a glass of wine.

As illustrated by these settings, spring is one of the loveliest of seasons to visit Amador County and the many wineries of Shenandoah Valley.

Fiddletown

Fiddletown was settled in 1849 by miners from Missouri who reportedly, when not mining, played their fiddles. Fiddletown was the setting for Bret Harte's "An Episode in Fiddletown."

Above. The Fiddletown General Store has been operating continuously since 1853.

Center. This rammed-earth adobe, built in the early 1850s, was the home of Chinese Doctors Yee Chew Kee and Chow Fong You. Many Chinese artifacts may be seen here in the museum.

Below. The impressive two story Schallorn Building dates to 1878.

Volcano

Volcano is an interesting town surrounded by hills on all sides. Extensive hydraulic mining was conducted in the area. On the east side of the main street are gold rush era buildings. On the west side only stone walls hint at structures from the past.

Above. The magnificent three story St. George Hotel, built in 1863, was preceded by two other structures dating to 1850. The hotel is one of only a few historic three story structures remaining in California's gold rush country.

Center. According to a plaque on the wall of the Kaiser General Store, a general store has operated on this site continuously since 1852.

Below. St. Bernard's Catholic Church dates to 1854.

Above. At Drytown, this brick building, dating to the 1850's, serves as both billboard and popular antique store. It is reported that William Randolph Hearst's father, George Hearst, operated a printing press and maintained his mining office in this building.

Below. At Amador City, the Amador Hotel dates to 1855. The Keystone Mine's head-frame stands on the hill above the town.

Opposite Page, Above, Left. At Indian Grinding Rock State Historic Park, between Volcano and Pine Grove, more than 1,185 chaw-ses (mortar cups) and numerous Indian drawings cover this huge rock. This was a locale visited by 49ers during the gold rush era.

Opposite Page, Above, Right. At Pine Grove, a huge maple and white picket fence remind the observer of New England scenes.

Opposite Page, Center, Left. At Daffodil Hill, the pioneer McLaughlin family has operated a nursery since 1877. They open their farm each spring to visitors who come to see the hillside of colorful flowers and their peacocks.

Opposite Page, Center, Right. Little remains of the gold rush town of Pioneer except for this graveyard.

Opposite Page, Below. At Pokerville, just west of Plymouth, this Chinese store survives.

In Memory of
NANCY
WIFE OF
J.B.KENDALL
DIED
June 20,1858;
Aged 41 Yrs.

Sutter Creek

Sutter Creek was named for John A. Sutter who first visited here in 1846 and later prospected in the nearby creeks in 1848. Sutter Creek is one of the most picturesque of the gold mining towns in California's gold rush country. The town's historic buildings line Highway 49. Sutter Creek was the site of the Old Eureka Mine, one of the most lucrative in the area. Leland J. Stanford, best known as the founder of Stanford University, Governor of California and co-builder of the Central Pacific Railroad, made much of his fortune from his investment in the Lincoln Mine just north of Sutter Creek. The historic Sutter Creek Methodist Church, right, was built in 1862.

Opposite Page, Above. *The Bellotti's Inn, built in 1867, is considered to be the oldest operating inn in California's gold rush country. Historic buildings of downtown Sutter Creek, right, include the Brignole Building, dating to 1856.*

Opposite Page, Center and Below. *The historic Sutter Creek Inn is built around a house that dates to 1859. Operator Jane Way sits among guests in the cozy parlor of this popular gold rush country inn.*

Above. *The Palace Restaurant occupies a saloon building that dates to 1897.*

Jackson

Jackson, the county seat for Amador County, was first called Botellas — Spanish for bottles — because of an abundance of bottles apparently discarded there by early travelers. Jackson reflects much of its ethnic diversity in the buildings that remain. Miners and emigrants who settled in the area include American, Mexican, Serbian and Italian.

Opposite Page, Above. *The historic National Hotel and I.O.O.F. building, both built in 1862, dominate the south end of Main Street. Much of the historic downtown area was destroyed in a major fire in 1862.*

Opposite Page, Below. *At Cafe Max, Saeval uses a brick oven that dates to 1865 to bake delicious pastries.*

Above. *The Amador County Museum is housed in the Armstead C. Brown House, which dates to 1859. Many artifacts from the gold rush era and the area are on display here.*

Below. *St. Patrick's Catholic Church, built in 1868, and its parsonage stand on the hill above downtown Jackson.*

163

Above. The Chichizola Store was built in 1850 at Jackson Gate. It serves today as an antique store where visitors can see the original safe and many reminders of its rich history.

Below. Nearby are the Kennedy Mine and its Tailings Wheels which dominate the landscape. The giant wheels, considered engineering marvels when constructed in 1905, were erected to move tailings from the Kennedy Mine over a hill into a tailing pond. The nearby Argonaut Mine, first operated in 1850, was closed during World War II. Both mines reached depths of more than 5,000 feet.

Opposite Page, Above. The Serbian Orthodox Church of St. Sava, built in 1894, represents but one example of the diverse cultural backgrounds of Jackson's settlers. St. Sava Church presents a picturesque setting as depicted in this series of pictures.

Opposite Page, Center, Right. The lone reminder of Butte City, the Ginocchio store, built in the early 1850s, sits just a few feet off Highway 49 south of Jackson. It appears to be perilously close to collapse.

Opposite Page, Below. Gardella's Inn, dating to the early 1850s when built at the edge of the Mokelumne River, is one of many inns constructed at Big Bar.

165

Calaveras County

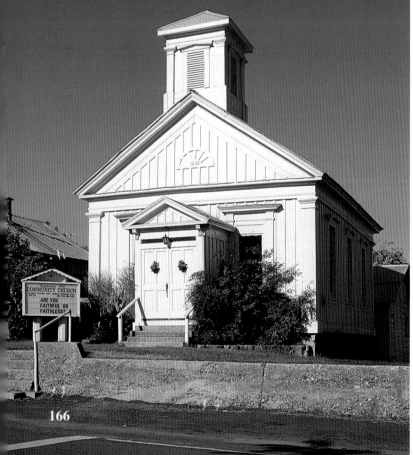

Calaveras County is known throughout the world, perhaps better than any of the other counties in California's gold rush country, because of the writings of Samuel Clemens and Bret Harte. Clemens, better known as Mark Twain, wrote his famous story, "The Celebrated Jumping Frog of Calaveras County," after visits to Angels Camp. Black Bart, one of the most legendary of the gold rush era bandits, began and ended his career in Calaveras County. In addition, the largest gold nugget in California's gold rush country, weighing in at 195 pounds, was discovered at Carson Hill.

Mokelumne Hill

Mokelumne Hill was one of the most important towns of the Southern Mines. It was reputed to be the wildest in California's gold rush country.

Page 166, Above. The dominant landmark in Mokelumne Hill is the historic Hotel Léger built in 1854. It has been well preserved and offers a delightful place for lunch, dinner or overnight stay. The former Calaveras County Courthouse, built in 1852, was incorporated into the Hotel Léger in 1866 when the county seat was relocated to San Andreas. To the right is French Hill, site of the so-called "French War" of 1851, where French and Americans fought over their diggins.

Page 166, Below, Left. This is the oldest Congregational Church building in California, dating from 1856.

Page 167, Below, Right. The L. Mayer & Son building, now in ruins, dates to 1854.

Opposite Page, Above. The three story I.O.O.F. Building first served as the Wells, Fargo & Company building when it was constructed in 1854 with two floors. The third floor was added in 1861 for use by the lodge.

Opposite Page, Below. The "China Gulch" street sign reminds visitors of the once large Chinese presence at Mokelumne Hill. Several miles south of Mokelumne Hill is Chili Gulch, named for the large population of Chileans who mined in this area.

Above. San Andreas was founded by Mexican miners in 1848. The Mexican bandit, Joaquin Murieta, was reported to operate in the area. San Andreas' historic district is located on North Main Street where its remaining historic buildings are clustered together. Gooney's Saloon building, right, was built in 1858. The building has served as a saloon, dry goods and hardware store. Adjacent to it is the Winkler Store, dating to 1858, which has been known as the Bartholemew, Crowley, Empire Bakery & Restaurant and the Post Office Building. The Cornell and Bowman Tinshop & Hardware store, built in 1857, stands next in line. The I.O.O.F. Building at San Andreas was constructed in 1856. The Hall of Records, built in 1893, is now the Calaveras County Museum and Visitors Center. The current Calaveras County Courthouse (not pictured but located behind the Hall of Records) was the setting for the trial of Black Bart. The famous stage coach robber, with a strong dislike for Wells, Fargo & Company, alias Black Bart (a.k.a. Charles Boles and Charles E. Bolton) was found guilty after a three day trial in November 1883.

Center. Only this ruin remains of the many buildings built at Jenny Lind in the gold rush era. Extensive dredging fields can be seen beside the nearby Stanislaus River.

Below. The Dughi Building was built at Mountain Ranch in the late 1860's by the Raggio and Dughi families. Nearby is the Domenghini building which began as a saloon in 1856.

169

California Caverns

Above. *At now defunct Cave City, guide Violet Rose shows Patrick Kelly the historic entrance to the Cave City Cave, now known as California Caverns. Operated by John Fairchild, tours explore the underground caverns where 49ers left behind their name and date of visit in the limestone rock walls.*

Below. *B. K. Thorn is credited with the capture of Black Bart. John Muir visited the Cave City Cave and wrote of his experiences there in **Mountains of California**. Bret Harte and Mark Twain are also reported to have visited Cave City.*

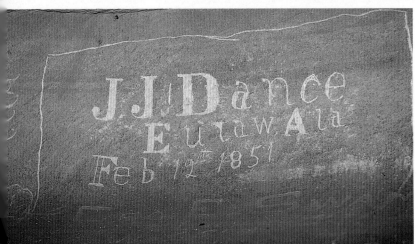

170

Sheep Ranch

Above. The Pioneer Hotel in Sheep Ranch began as a one story hotel in Cheechee Flats in the 1870s. It was moved to Sheep Ranch in 1904 where the second floor was added. The nearby Sheep Ranch Mine was owned by Senator George Hearst, father of Randolph William Hearst. Hearst used his father's gold fortune to establish the Hearst Newspapers.

Center. Sheep have their run on the streets of Sheep Ranch.

Below. The General Store is a dominant feature on Main Street in Sheep Ranch.

Calaveritas

Above. *The Old Costa Store dates to 1852, according to the matriarch of the family, Louise Greenlaw.*

Center and Below. *A small adobe house behind the store is older although the exact date of its construction is unknown. Both are on private land and are not open to the public.*

Above. At Douglas Flat, the school house dates to 1854. Scars on the hillside behind the school house indicate hydraulic mining activity. Douglas Flat was on the Central Hill Channel, an ancient river deposit which was rich in gold.

Center, Left. The Gilleado (or Gilieardo) Building, reportedly built in 1851, was used as a store and bank at Douglas Flat.

Center, Right. At Vallecito, this bell formerly hung in a nearby tree and was rung each Sunday to summon parishioners to church service.

Below. The Dinkelspiel Store, built in 1851 at Vallecito, was used until just a few years ago.

Murphys

Murphys, known as the Queen of the Sierra, is one of the few gold rush towns of any size not on California's Highway 49. Possibly because of this, it has retained much of its original charm and many of its historic buildings. Most of its earliest buildings were lost in a fire that swept the town in 1859. Murphys (also known as Murphys Flat and Murphys Diggins) was named after brothers Daniel and John Murphy who arrived here in 1848. They set up a trading post and first mined along Angels Creek which runs through the town.

Above and Below, Left. *The Murphys Hotel was first built in 1856 as the Sperry and Perry's Hotel. It burned, along with most of the other buildings in town, in 1859. When rebuilt in 1860, it was named The Murphys Hotel. Famous guests who stayed here have included Mark Twain, Horatio Algier, U. S. Grant and C. E. Bolton (alias Black Bart).*

Center, Right. *The Vassaelo/Ruiseco & Orengo/Segale Store was built in 1859. Lower, center. The Heinsdorff/Thorpe Bakery building, built in 1851, has two-foot-thick walls which have helped it to survive fires.*

Lower, Right. *The Bonnet/Compere Store, one of the prettiest stone structures in all of California's gold rush country, was built of rhyolite blocks and limestone rubble in 1858.*

174

Above. The Peter L. Traver Building, right, built in 1856, was one of a few buildings to survive the 1859 fire. The building is now the home of the Old-Timers Museum. The Thompson Building, left, was constructed in 1862. There are a number of plaques on its side wall, called the Wall of Comparative Ovations of E Clampus Vitus. Among the plaques (*Below, Left*) is this drawing of Joseph Zumwalt who founded ECV and (*Center, Right*) a drawing that depicts the often tenuous relationship between 49ers and their donkeys.

Below, Right. A number of comfortable Bed and Breakfasts have been established in historic houses at Murphys. Among them is the Dunbar House which dates to 1880.

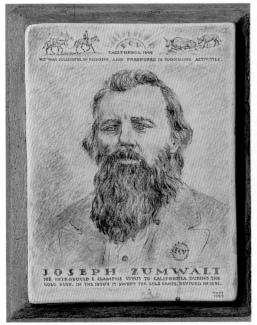

Altaville

Altaville, founded in 1852, is usually remembered as the site for an apparent hoax involving the so-called Calaveras Skull "discovered" in the Mattison Mine in 1866. There are two well preserved buildings at Altaville from the gold rush era.

Above. The Altaville Grammar School, built in 1858, stands in a shady grove of trees beside Highway 49. The school was constructed with funds raised from a dance held at the nearby Prince and Garibardi Building.

Below. The two story Prince and Garibardi Building, still used as a commercial building, dates to 1857.

Angels Camp

Angels Camp was named for Henry Angel, the town's first store keeper. The Utica Mine was the most famous of the area's mines, producing until 1942. There were more than 200 stamp mills operating around the clock at Angels Camp during the period 1880 and 1890. Local legend says that when they ceased operating, the town was so quiet that people could not sleep.

Above. On the right is the Angels Hotel which dates to 1855. Mark Twain, who lived at nearby Jackass Hill in Tuolumne County during the years 1864 and 1865, visited Angels Camp and its diggins. It was at the Angels Hotel that Ross Coon, the proprietor, told Mark Twain the story that he later embellished and wrote as "The Celebrated Jumping Frog of Calaveras County."

Below. Angels Camp has a thriving downtown reminiscent of its heyday during the gold rush era. A number of gold rush era buildings remain here, including the E. & G. Stickle Building (1856) and the I.O.O.F. Building (1860).

177

Even though Mark Twain was an accomplished writer, it was his short story, **The Celebrated Jumping Frog of Calaveras County**, first published in the **New York Saturday Press**, that brought him fame. The first Jumping Frog Jubilee was held in 1928 to celebrate the paving of Main Street in Angels Camp in a style commemorative of its gold rush heritage. The winner was Pride of San Joaquin with a jump of three feet and six inches. Calaveras County has since celebrated Mark Twain's famous story with yearly events now held at the Calaveras County Fairgrounds at nearby Frogtown. These pictures were taken during the 1995 event.

WORLDS RECORD 21.5¾ IN. SET BY "ROSIE THE RIBITER" JOCKEY, LEE GIUDICI

Above, Left. *Tom Sawyer and Becky Thatcher of Hannibal, Missouri, are yearly visitors to The Jumping Frog Jubilee. This year they were represented by Grant Evert and Whitney Locke.*

Below, Left. *Crystal Oldfield of nearby Mountain Ranch urges her frog to make a record setting jump.*

Above. *The Jumping Frog Jubilee offers many attractions, from this sand sculpture of frogs and horses to the Budweiser Clydesdales (left of the stage).*

Center. *A frog is about to be dropped onto the "jump pad."*

Below, Right. *This frog, urged on by its owner, makes a mighty leap.*

179

Above. Calaveras County is often described by residents as a number of quiet towns with lots of country in between. These sheep are on a farm near Angels Camp.

Left. Colorful fall foliage provides a golden cast to Angels Creek, reminiscent of its heyday when miners lined the creek seeking "the color."

Below, Right. The Angels Camp Museum, on the north side of Angels Camp, houses many interesting artifacts from the gold rush era.

Opposite Page, Above. The Romaggi House, dating to 1856, sits quietly beside Highway 49 about two miles south of Angels Camp.

Opposite Page, Center. Carson Hill is the site where, in 1854, the largest gold nugget in California's gold rush country was found. The nugget weighed 195 pounds. Mining operations continue here today. (Aerial photography of Carson Hill © 1995 by Patrick T. Kelly)

Opposite Page, Below. The New Melones Reservoir has covered over the site of Robinson's Ferry which provided passage across the Stanislaus River during the gold rush era.

180

181

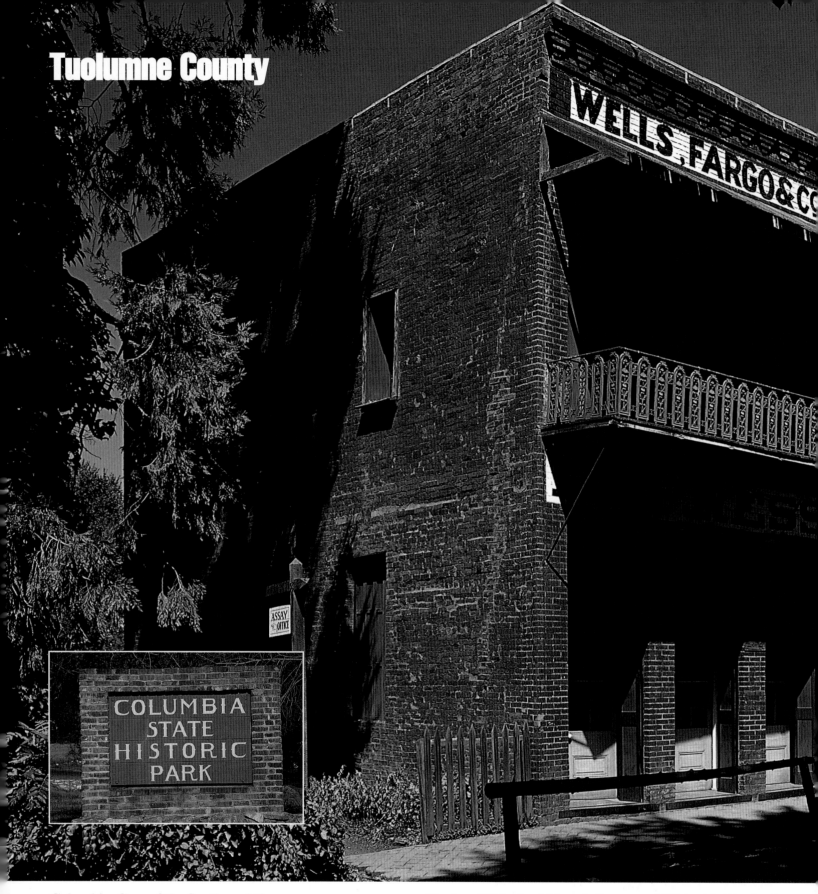

Columbia, Gem of the Southern Mines

Known as the "Gem of the Southern Mines," Columbia's role in the gold rush and its historic importance today in California's gold rush country is second only to that of Coloma. With more than 250 acres incorporated into the Columbia State Historic Park, visitors are afforded the opportunity to vicariously experience the gold rush era. Visitors can ride an authentic stagecoach, stay in an old hotel and shop in gold rush era stores.

Gold was discovered at Columbia on March 27, 1850 by Dr. Thadeus Hildreth. Although first named Hildreth's Diggins for its discoverer, the town was soon called Columbia. Columbia grew to a town of more than 5,000 people with 150 saloons, shops and stores and other businesses catering to the gold miners. Following fires which swept through Columbia in 1854 and 1857, the town was rebuilt with fireproof brick and iron "fire doors."

Columbia proved to be the richest area in California's gold rush country. More than $1.5 billion in gold, at today's prices, was removed from the area around Columbia. The huge rocks

that surround Columbia, almost surreal in appearance, were exposed as miners removed topsoil to a depth of approximately sixty feet. Columbia was originally a "dry diggins". When water was finally brought to Columbia in 1853, sluice operations speeded up the removal of gold rich topsoil.

In 1945, the State of California purchased Columbia and established it as the Columbia State Historic Park. Columbia is the best preserved of all of the old mining towns in California's gold rush country.

Left. *The Wells, Fargo & Company building, built in 1858, is the dominant building in Columbia State Historic Park. More than 1.4 million ounces of gold were weighed in on the scales on display at the Wells Fargo & Company office here. Stagecoaches regularly departed from Columbia for San Francisco, Mariposa and Placerville.*

Inset. *A favorite of visitors to Columbia State Historic Park, this authentic stagecoach operates through the streets and the nearby "canyon area" of the diggins. Stagecoach service at Columbia State Historic Park is now provided by Columbia Stage Line and Stable.*

Above. Columbia Firehouse #1, an ornate structure on Main Street, features period fire fighting equipment centered around the Old Monumental fire engine.

Center. The Columbia Livery houses period exhibits while the adjacent (not pictured) blacksmith shop provides smithing activity reminiscent of the days when horsepower was the means of travel.

Below. The Wells, Fargo & Company office appears today much as it did when constructed in 1858.

Above. A visitor stops to smell the flowers in front of Columbia Firehouse #1.

Below, Right. Columbia's small jail house has an imposing steel door that was used to keep law breakers behind bars.

The City Hotel was first built in 1856 and known as the What Cheer House. A fire destroyed the structure in 1857. Rebuilt in 1871, the hotel has been known as The City Hotel since 1874. In addition to providing excellent hotel and restaurant services reminiscent of California's gold rush era, The City Hotel serves as a training center for Columbia College's Hospitality Management Program. Managed by Tom Bender,

The City Hotel is noted throughout California's gold rush country for first class service and its fine cuisine prepared and served by students from Columbia College, with assistance from professional staff.

Opposite Page. Here, served by Kathi Harvey, Cathy Carradus and Les Kelly enjoy a gourmet meal at The City Hotel. The drawing on the wall depicts Columbia in 1855, as seen from Kennebec Hill.

Above. The Masonic Hall, left, reconstructed in 1949 to replace an earlier three story building built in 1854, is an excellent example of restoration at Columbia State Historic Park. The Fallon Hotel, right, was built in 1859. The Fallon Hotel Theatre serves as the stage for the Columbia Actors' Repertory. With support from Columbia College, CAR offers eight major productions during the annual twelve-month season.

Below. The Columbia Museum depicts local period history through exhibits and displays.

Opposite Page, Above. The Brady Building dates to 1899. Visitors can buy gold rush era items as well as tourist souvenirs.

Opposite Page, Center. Visitors stroll along Main Street in Columbia.

Opposite Page, Below. Rocks in the Canyon area around Columbia rise high above Jim "Arthritis" Christiensen (left) and Pete Lawson. Before miners dug for gold here, these rocks were buried deep below the topsoil.

189

Papeete, the fire engine that is the pride of the Columbia Volunteer Fire Department, was built in 1852 for the King of Tahiti. Discovered abandoned on a ship in the San Francisco Harbor in 1859, it has served Columbia well since that time. Here, in the 1995 Fireman's Muster, Papeete throws water further than the other historic pumpers.

Inset, Top. The yearly Fireman's Muster is a festive occasion as depicted here with local Boy Scouts leading the parade.

Inset, Left. Old Monumental, housed in Columbia Firehouse #1, won the trophy for "best of historic" class.

Inset, Right, Above. Papeete stands proudly in front of Firehouse #2, where it is on permanent display.

Photograph courtesy of Columbia Volunteer Fire Department and Stan Steiner.

Above. St. Ann's Church is situated on Kennebec Hill above the southern edge of Columbia. The cemetery has tombstones dating from 1852. Exquisite paintings decorate the interior of this pioneer church which was built in 1856.

Below. This replica cabin stands on Jackass Hill at the site of the Gillis Brothers' cabin where Mark Twain stayed in 1864-1865. The chimney is reported to be authentic to the original cabin built by the Gillises.

Sonora

Sonora, also known as Sonorian Camp, was founded by Mexicans and is referred to as the "Queen of the Southern Mines". Sonora's mines proved to be among the richest in California's gold rush country.

Above. The St. James Church, also known as the "Red Church," stands on Piety Hill in Sonora. The church, which dates to 1859, is considered to be the most scenic and is perhaps the most photographed in all of California's gold rush country. The Bonanza Mine, also on Piety Hill, proved to be the largest and richest pocket mine in California's gold rush country.

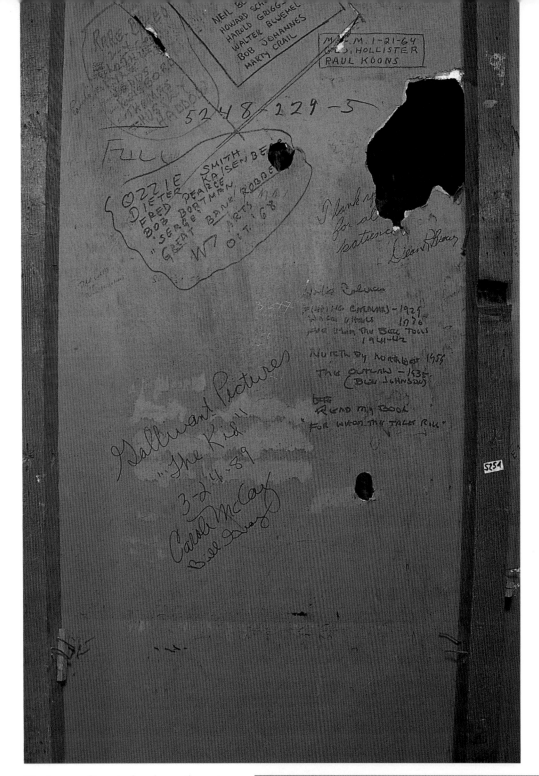

Tuolumne County has been the setting for more than 300 movies and television shows since 1919 when Universal Pictures filmed segments of **The Red Glove** near Sonora. Movies filmed in Tuolumne County at Columbia, Sonora and Jamestown, include **High Noon** (1952), **For Whom the Bell Tolls** (1943), **Apache** (1954), **Big Country** (1958), **Dodge City** (1939) and **The Virginian** (1924). More recently, it has served as the setting for **Back to the Future III**, Clint Eastwood's **Unforgiven** and **The Great American West**. While these films are a part of contemporary history, all are set in a historic period reminiscent of the gold rush era.

Opposite Page, Above, Left. *This wall, part of a small darkroom built into a corner of the basement of The Sonora Inn, served as a bulletin board to crews who worked on the films.*

Opposite Page, Below. *The City Hotel, built in 1852 as an adobe structure, is a prominent feature on Washington Street in Sonora. The hotel now houses offices and shops.*

Above. *The Sonora Inn dates to 1896 when it opened as the Hotel Victoria. After a fire in 1923 destroyed much of its façade, it was remodeled and opened as The Sonora Inn in 1931. Clint Eastwood reportedly favors The Sonora Inn when he is in town. Sonora's movie heritage is celebrated yearly in September with the Tuolumne County Wild West Film Fest.*

Below, Right. *Sonora, painted in many colors as seen from Knowles Hill, is one of the most scenic towns in California's gold rush country.*

Opposite Page. The Tuolumne County Museum is housed in the former county jailhouse which was built in 1865. Extensive exhibits present county history, the gold rush era and the Overland Trails which crossed the Sierra Nevada.

Above. The Gunn House is the oldest surviving building in Sonora. The original two story adobe structure, built in 1850, has been incorporated into a delightful hotel, with an excellent restaurant. In addition, the Gunn House served as the office for the Sonora Herald, the first newspaper published in California's gold rush country. The first edition was published on July 4, 1850.

Below, Left. Numerous shops in old buildings along Washington Street make downtown Sonora an interesting place to shop.

Below, Right. The Street-Morgan Mansion, built in 1896, stands at the top of Piety Hill, at the northern end of Washington Street.

Jamestown

Jamestown got its name from a lawyer who settled here in 1848. Locals often prefer to call it Jimtown.

Above. The Emporium, dating from 1897, dominates downtown Jamestown. Across the street is The National Hotel, built in 1859. The National Hotel is well known for its food and wine festivals.

Center. Numerous businesses offer visitors the opportunity to try their luck at mining for gold.

Below. Table Mountain, a flat lava ridge, dominates the skyline from Columbia to Knight's Ferry. A number of mines operated very successfully in and around Table Mountain.

Opposite Page, Above. The Jimtown 1849 Gold Mining Camp operates on Wood's Creek in Jamestown. The Jamestown Players recreate a scene typical of gold rush days.

Opposite Page, Below. The Jamestown United Methodist Church was built in 1852. Church records note that it was "Built and paid for in 1852 partly by the gamblers and partly by the good people of Jamestown for the use of all sects on Sundays and for educational purposes on week days."

The Sierra Railway has been a popular setting for many movies including the long running television show Petticoat Junction. The Sierra Railway's Engine No. 3 was a familiar sight in Hooterville. The railroad's twenty-six acre complex is now preserved as Railtown 1897 in Jamestown. The railway's large collection of rolling stock and its roundtable make it a favorite setting for western theme movies. Visitors are welcome to tour the museum and take train rides.

Opposite Page, Below. Table Mountain stands above the surrounding pasture land near Chinese Camp.

Below. Two old rock corrals are still used near Chinese Camp, left, and at the site of Crimea House, right.

Chinese Camp

Above. *The McAdams Store, built in 1854, now serves as the Headquarters for the Tuolumne County Visitor Bureau at Chinese Camp. The store is across the street from the ruins of the Wells, Fargo & Company building which consists of a small portion of the original adobe wall. Five thousand Chinese mined here at the peak of activity.*

Below. *The picturesque St. Francis Xavier Catholic Church, dating to 1854, stands on a hill above Chinese Camp.*

Don Pedro Lake is the largest and one of the most used recreation areas in California's gold rush country. The lake's first dam was constructed in 1923. The current dam, made of rocks and earth, was constructed in 1971 by the City and County of San Francisco, the Turlock Irrigation District and the Modesto Irrigation District.

Big Oak Flat

Above. *The I.O.O.F. Building at Big Oak Flat, built in 1853, is still used for local social activities.*

Below. *This old building, near the I.O.O.F. Building, dates to the early 1850's.*

Groveland

Opposite Page, Above. *The Groveland Hotel, left, was built in 1849. The thick adobe walls are of Monterey Colonial Architectural Style. Beautifully restored, The Groveland Hotel's rooms are charming and the food is excellent. An addition was constructed in 1914 to accommodate workers on the nearby O'Shaughnessy Dam project. The dam project created a reservoir in the Hetch Hetchy Valley to supply water and electricity for San Francisco. The Iron Door Saloon, built prior to 1852, is the oldest saloon in California's gold rush country. The saloon is named for its massive iron doors which were shipped around Cape Horn from England*

Opposite Page, Below. *The Moccasin Powerhouse, on Moccasin Creek, a part of the Hetch Hetchy project, provides electricity for San Francisco.*

204

205

There are many scenic settings in California's gold rush country. For this photographer, one hill provided a changing panorama of beauty. In each of these three settings, located just south of the Moccasin Powerhouse, Moccasin Creek flows through the lower portion of the scene behind a screen of shrubs and trees.

Above. *Spring "foliage" colors the deciduous trees and shrubs, while fall foliage (**Below**) paints a picturesque setting.*

Opposite Page. *Summer flowers and green trees under wispy cirrus clouds create a beautiful summer tapestry.*

Stanislaus County

La Grange

The small town of La Grange, is situated on the banks of the Tuolumne River.

Above. *In the downtown area are a number of historic structures, the most prominent of which is The Trading Post built in 1850-1851.*

Center. *A bucket from the nearby La Grange Dredge is displayed in front of The Trading Post.*

Knight's Ferry

Below. *At Knight's Ferry, the longest covered bridge in the west has carried traffic across the Stanislaus River since 1864. The bridge replaced an earlier bridge built in 1854 which in turn had replaced a ferry operated since 1850 near this spot. Knight's Ferry was an important river crossing on the road from Stockton to Sonora and the southern mines. The Army Corps of Engineers, which has responsibility for the bridge, hired the late Milton Graton of New Hampshire to restore the bridge in the late 1980s. When he finished his work, Graton, known as "The Last of the Covered Bridge Builders," advised the author that the bridge was good for another 100 years! To the left of*

the bridge is the office building, dating to 1863, for the old flour mill that operated here.

Above and Right, Below, Right. *This dredger operated in the Tuolumne River in the early 1940's. The dredger's apparent final resting place is a small pond off Highway 59 near La Grange. Huge piles of rocks along the nearby banks of the Tuolumne River were pulled from the river by this rusting dredger.*

Below, Left. *Nearby, in the town of Knight's Ferry, the oldest general store in all of California's gold rush country has operated continuously since 1852. Bridge builder John Dent's house, constructed in 1851, still stands on Ellen Street.*

Mariposa County

Coulterville

Mariposa means "butterfly" in Spanish. When created in 1850, Mariposa County covered one-fifth of California and was the largest county ever created in the United States. Today, after being carved up to create an additional eleven counties, it has approximately 17,000 residents. Mariposa County is distinguished as being the gateway to Yosemite, the major tourist destination in California's gold rush country since its "final discovery" in 1851 by Major James D. Savage. Founded in 1850 by George W. Coulter, Coulterville remains a small town in a picturesque setting with few changes since the discovery of gold. A number of its historic structures remain, some still in everyday use. The entire town of Coulterville has been designated as a State Historical Landmark. The Jeffery Hotel is the dominant landmark at the intersection of Highways 49 and 132.

Above. *Ruins of the Coulterville Hotel, left, the Wells, Fargo & Company building, built in 1856, and McCarthy's store now serve as the Northern Mariposa County History Center. Nelson Cody, brother of "Buffalo Bill" Cody, served as agent and postmaster here in the 1870's. Whistling Billy, a narrow gauge engine used in the nearby Mary Harrison Mine, rests under Coulterville's hangin' tree.*

Opposite Page, Below, Left. *The entrance to the Northern Mariposa County History Center is framed by colorful flowers while the Hotel Jeffrey dominates the skyline.*

Below, Right. *The Sun Sun Wo Company building was constructed of adobe in 1851 to serve the Chinese community which numbered more than one thousand during gold rush days.*

Above. *Operated by Karin Fielding and Louis Bickford, the Jeffery Hotel, with the attached Magnolia Saloon, offers visitors a comfortable stay in a structure little altered since its construction in 1851. The hotel's construction and appearance bear tribute to the influence of Mexicans who were first in the area.*

Center and Below. *Patrons enjoy talk and drinks or play a game of pool in the Magnolia Saloon, one of the oldest bars in California's gold rush country.*

Opposite Page. *Spring is especially lovely in Mariposa County. Here, a red bud tree blooms beside Highway 49 which winds through Hell's Hollow, south of Coulterville.*

Above. Hell's Hollow is one of the most impressive sights along California's Highway 49. The highway drops almost 1,000 feet down to Lake McClure in the valley below.

Below, Left. Lake McClure now covers the site of Bagby where the Merced River crosses Highway 49. A modern dredger is used here to mine for gold.

Below, Right. Venus lights up the early morning sky at Hell's Hollow.

Bear Valley

Bear Valley was established by General John C. Frémont who bought a "floating land grant" in 1849 for $3,000. Named "Rancho Las Mariposas," it consisted of 44,000 acres with headquarters here. When gold was discovered on his lands, he "floated" the boundaries to include much of the gold fields in the area. His claims were challenged in one of the landmark cases regarding mining claims. He won his case in the nearby Mariposa County Courthouse in 1856. During the gold rush years of 1850 to 1860, there were as many as 3,000 miners in the Bear Valley area. Frémont sold his lands by 1860 for $6 million.

Above. The fast disappearing ruins of the Gagliardo Store, dating to the early 1850's, at Bear Valley are just off Highway 49.

Below. The Bon Ton Café dates to 1860 when it was a saloon. It has also housed the Wells, Fargo & Company office. The crumbling walls of the Frémont Store, left, are all that remain of the building constructed in the early 1850's. The stone building, right, housed the offices of the Mariposa Mining Company, owned by Frederick Law Olmsted who purchased much of the land grant from Frémont.

Hornitos

Hornitos was patterned after Mexican villages with a town plaza surrounded by saloons and shops. Many of its early settlers are believed to have come from Sonora, Mexico. Its name is thought to originate with the small ovens used to cook and bake or from the above ground oven like tombs in the Hornitos cemetery. What is clear, however, is that rowdy and violent miners, thrown out of nearby Quartzburg in 1850, moved to Hornitos along with attendant gambling dens, brothels and saloons. Hornitos was known as one of the richest and roughest mining camps in the Southern Mines. The notorious Mexican bandit, Joaquin Murieta, visited here frequently, when not conducting raids throughout California's gold rush country. Considerable gold was mined from Hornitos Creek. Its most famous resident, Domingo Ghirardelli, set up shop here in 1849. He made his stake and then moved to San Francisco in 1852 to establish his famous Ghirardelli's Chocolate Factory. A number of historic buildings remain around the Plaza and Main Street in Hornitos. Hornitos is distinguished as the only incorporated town (1870) in Mariposa County. During its heyday, there were 15,000 citizens, 12 hotels and 36 saloons. Today, Hornitos is a quiet village with less than 75 residents. Among the numerous buildings and ruins to be seen in Hornitos are the I.O.O.F. and Masonic Building, built in 1860 *(Lower, Left)*, the Hornitos Jail, built in 1849 and the oldest remaining structure, *(Lower, Right)*, the St. Catherine's Catholic Church on the hill above town dates to 1869 *(Opposite Page, Lower, Left)* and this ruin at the edge of town *(Opposite Page, Lower, Right)*. The Gagliardo & Company *(Inset Above)* was established in 1852 or 1853.

Above. *The Quick Ranch at Ben Hur dates to 1859. Ranch buildings lie just over the hill in this picture. The stone fence, a portion of which is seen here, was built by Chinese laborers in 1862 and is five miles in length.*

Opposite Page, Left. *The small Pioneer Cemetery at Ben Hur is filled with spring flowers.*

Below. *Rolling hills and rushing creeks make Mariposa County one of the loveliest in California's gold rush country.*

Mariposa

In the downtown area of Mariposa, a number of buildings remain from the gold rush era. Like the other towns in California's gold rush country, Mariposa suffered destructive fires in 1858 and 1866. Gold was discovered in Mariposa Creek which runs the length of Mariposa.

Above. The I.O.O.F. building, left, was constructed in 1866. At the far end of the block, right, stands the Schlageter Hotel built in 1866.

Below. The oldest church in Mariposa, St. Joseph's Church, built in 1861, sits on the hill above the southern entrance to Mariposa.

Above. The Mariposa County Courthouse, built in 1854, is one of California's most historic buildings. The second courthouse to serve Mariposa County, it is the oldest courthouse in continuous use in California and west of the Mississippi River. The courthouse was constructed by P. V. Fox and A. F. Shriver for $9,000 from white pine from a nearby grove. When the cupola and clock were added in 1866, the local newspaper, The Mariposa Gazette, first published in 1854, predicted problems: "It will be a very extra affair, the courthouse ain't fenced in and how unfortunate if some of the scores of hogs that have their nests around there, should poke their nose under the corners and shake the pendulum off the time."

Below. Visitors to the courtroom will note that the spectator's benches, the jury box and the judge's bench still bear the marks of Fox and Shriver's carpenter's plane. The important Frémont case and others were argued in this courtroom. Jury decisions here determined much of the law that governs mining operations in the western states today.

Mariposa is rich in museums, which preserve the history of the area and display relics of California's gold rush.

Above. *The Mariposa Museum and History Center has displays which include a five-stamp mill, a typical one-room miner's cabin and much information about John C. Frémont, who played a major role in opening up the west, establishing statehood for California and development of Mariposa County. Also included is an interesting display of the interior of the Gagliardo Store from Hornitos.*

Center and Below. *The Fricot Nugget, a piece of crystallized gold from El Dorado County, is one of the major displays housed by the California State Mining and Mineral Museum. Adjacent to the Mariposa County Fairgrounds, the museum houses the State of California's historic gem and mineral collection. Nearby is the site of Mormon Bar, discovered in 1849 by members of the Mormon Battalion.*

Right. The highway and railroad along the Merced River were important links to Yosemite.

Below. Although the Yosemite Valley was visited by earlier explorers, it was not until 1851, when Major James D. Savage and Captain John Boling led members of the "Mariposa Battalion" into the valley in pursuit of marauding Indians, that Yosemite became well known. Many 49ers visited California's best known natural landmark.

Bodie

Named for William S. Bodey who found gold here in 1859, Bodie is the best known "ghost town" in California's gold rush country. Incorporated into the Bodie State Historic Park in 1962, it is maintained in a state of "arrested decay." By 1880, there were 10,000 people in Bodie, and the town was well known for frequent killings and wickedness. It is reported that one young girl, upon learning that she was going to Bodie with her family, wrote: "Goodbye God, I'm going to Bodie."

Above. *Gold rush aficionados, left to right, Ed Cooper, Delia McClintock, Todd Frazier, Linda Ward, Dave Rosenberger and Tom Murray pose around an old grave in the Bodie Cemetery to "mourn" the passing of a friend. In*

the background is Bodie and the Standard Mine.

Inset, Above. A later addition to Bodie was this Twentieth Century gas station. In the background is the stamping mill of the Standard Mine.

Inset, Below. Some 168 buildings still remain at Bodie in various states of deterioration. The dry air of the high Sierra has helped slow the rate of deterioration of the buildings.

225

Above. *The Methodist Church, built in 1882, is the only church that remains in Bodie.*

Center. *Members of the Bodie Chapter of E Clampus Vitus celebrate the placement of this marker at the Bridgeport Inn, in Bridgeport, in 1994. Many markers noting the historic importance of old buildings have been erected by the fun loving ECV throughout California's gold rush country.*

Below. *The Mono County Courthouse in Bridgeport was built in 1880.*

Acknowledgements

Special thanks go to the following people who assisted me with specific information during my trips to and through California's gold rush country:

Alleghany: Elyse Ludiam, 16-1 Mining Company; Angels Camp: Carol Cook, Calaveras County Fair & Jumping Frog Jubilee, Nancy Larson, Angels Camp Museum; Auburn: Val Clark, Placer County Visitor Information Center, Hal Hall, Placer County Historical Society; Berkeley: William Roberts, The Bancroft Library; Blairsden: Ranger Mike Krause, Plumas-Eureka State Park; Bodie: Brad Sturdivant, Bodie State Historic Park; Brown's Valley: Paul and Lynne Bukenhoff; Calaveritas: Louise Greenlaw; Challenge: Dennis Woll; Chico: Ranger William B. Steward, Bidwell Mansion State Historic Park; Coloma: Alan Beilharz, John Hutchinson, Ron McCall, Barbara and David Thomas; Columbia: Stan Steiner, Violet Rose; Copperopolis: Traci Morrison; Coulterville: Billie Jenkins, Karin Fielding, Hotel Jeffrey; Downieville: Donald S. Russell, The Mountain Messenger; Folsom: Linda Swenson, American River State Recreation Area; Frenchtown: Dale Mozley; Georgetown: Connie Millman, Will Collin; Grass Valley: Peggy Levine, The Holbrooke Hotel, Donna Jones and Jane Hall, Empire Mine State Historic Park, Randy Spears, Larry Markey and Terry Mayfield, Nevada Irrigation District; Groveland: Grover and Peggy A. Mosley, The Groveland Hotel, Drew Knowles, Sandy Golden and Bob De Carlin, Iron Door Saloon; Jackson: Saeval; Jamestown: Larry Ingold, Railtown 1897, Stephen Willey, The National Hotel; LaGrange: Billee Zanker, LaGrange Museum Society; Kelsey: Sheley Little; Knight's Ferry: Lisa Vaccaro, Army Corps of Engineers; Loyalton: Juanita Shelton, Sierra County Chamber of Commerce; Mariposa: Shirley Mitchell, California State Mining & Mineral Museum, Dixie Trabucco, Scott Pinkerton; Marysville: Chuck Smith; Mountain Ranch: John Fairchild, California Caverns; Murphys: Jan Olson, Black Sheep Winery; Nevada City: Ed Tyson, Searles Library, Barbara Weaver, Firehouse Museum #1; North Bloomfield: Ranger Ken Huie, Malakoff Diggins State Historic Park; Placerville: Shirley Richards, El Dorado County Chamber of Commerce; Plymouth: Lee Sobon, Shenandoah Vineyards; Quincy: Linda Brennan, Plumas County Museum; Rich Bar: Norman Grant; Sacramento: Bob Basura, Sutter's Fort State Historic Park, Sheryl Gonzalez, Crocker Art Museum, Carol Cullens and Linda McDonald, California Department of Parks and Recreation, Publications Unit, Dahlynn Shiflet, Jack Steed, Robert A. Young, Senior Photographer, California Department of Parks and Recreation; San Andreas: Cheryl Waller, Calaveras County Historical Society; San Francisco: Joi Deager, Macy's, Jackie Flynn, Boudin Bakery; Sonora: Vincent Hoss, Sonora Inn, Christopher Link, Peggy and Van A. Schoell, Gunn House Hotel; Sutter Creek: Jane Way, Sutter Creek Inn; Volcano: Marlene Inman, St. George Hotel; Washington: Colin Haughin, Trading Post Cafe; Weaverville, Patricia Hicks; Wheatland: John Eachus, Damon Ranch.

For help with the segment on The Way West, thanks are due to, Idaho: Kathleen Durfee, City of Rocks National Reserve, Almo; Kansas: Duane Durst, Hollenberg Station State Historic Site, Hanover, Jack Haller, Alcove Springs Preservation Association, Blue Rapids; Missouri: John Mark Lambertson, National Frontier Trails Center, Independence, Jeanne Miller, Oregon-California Trails Association, Independence, Nancy Stuenkel, Hannibal Chamber of Commerce, Hannibal; Nebraska, Susan Berryman,

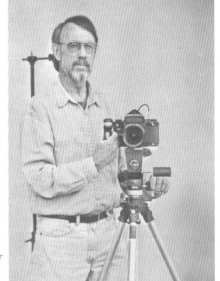

Early photographers recorded many activities and places throughout California's gold rush country that help preserve this important event at the sesquicentennial of California's gold rush. It was estimated in 1860 by early photographer Marcus Aurelius Root that there were approximately 10,000 working photographers in America. Bill Dunniway, owner of William Dunniway & Company, Mount Hermon, California, used the wet-plate collodion process, also called tin-type, to create this black and white portrait of the author at Coloma. The headrest used to "hold" subjects in place has been deliberately exposed to show one of the early photographer's tools of trade.

Dunniway, with his assistant, uses his 1860s E. & H.T. Anthony Co. camera-box to photograph a costumed participant in the Gold Mining Championships at Coloma.

Nebraska Division of Travel and Tourism, Lincoln, Charles Holthus, Lisco, Dean Knudsen, Scotts Bluff National Monument, Gering, Lonnie Logan, Stewards of the Platte, Grand Island, Eli Paul and John Carter, Nebraska State Historical Society, Lincoln, Loren Pospisil, Chimney Rock Visitor Center, Bayard; Utah: Brad Probst, This is the Place State Park, Salt Lake City; Wyoming: Dr. Roger P. Blair, MD, Sheridan, Richard L. Young, Fort Caspar Museum, Casper.

In the Republic of Panama, for the crossing of the Isthmus, assistance was provided by the Panama Canal Commission, Balboa: Willie K. Friar, Melvin D. Kennedy, Paul Reed and Jaime Robleto; Captain Leo Critides, Argonaut International, S.A., Balboa; Dr. Percy Núñez, Panamá; Willy Hector Vermaza, Panamá; and, Javier Romero and Ana Maríe Palm, Aventuras Panamá.

Horses and stagecoach at Columbia courtesy of Davy Stoller, Columbia Stage Line & Stables. Mariposa County Courthouse history courtesy of Mariposa County Chamber of Commerce, information provided by Scott Pinkerton. "That Bourn From Which No Traveler Returns: Cholera and the Overland Experience", Roger P. Blair, M.D., Sheridan, Wyoming. History of Coloma and James W. Marshall excerpted from *The Gold Discovery*, California Department of Parks and Recreation, used with Permission of Marshall Gold Discovery State Historic Park. Tin-type courtesy of Bill Dunniway, William Dunniway & Company, P.O. Box 443, Mount Hermon, CA 95041-0443; (408) 338-9473.

For more information about California's gold rush country, we recommend:

Traveling California's Gold Rush Country, Falcon Press, Leslie A. Kelly. This book provides travel information for those who wish to visit the sites and places written about in *California's Gold Rush Country*. *Historic Spots in California*, Stanford University Press. An excellent resource, this book was first written in 1932 by Mildred Brooke Hoover, Hero Eugene Rensch, Ethel Grace Rensch; updated in 1968 by William N. Abeloe with maps and excellent cross reference; current edition by Douglas E. Kyle; *The California Gold Rush Diary of a German Sailor* (Adolphus Windeler) edited by W. Turrentine Jackson; *The California Trail, Yesterday and Today*, written and illustrated by William E. Hill; *The Donner Party Rescue Site* by Jack Steed; *The Gold Discovery Journal of Azariah Smith* edited by David Bigler; *The World Rushed In* by J. S. Holliday; *The Shirley Letters* by Louise Clappe; *They Saw the Elephant, Women in the California Gold Rush* by Joann Levy; *What I Saw in California* by Edwin Bryant; *Six Months in the Gold Mines* by Edward Gould Buffum.

Below. Sherrin Grout, Ranger at Columbia State Historic Park, is one of the many officers who make a visit to California's State Parks both pleasant and informative.

Appendix

16-1 Mine, 93
40 Mile Desert, 24, 41
49ers, 12, 14, 24, 26, 27, 30, 33, 38, 39, 41-43, 46-48, 52, 62, 70, 88, 96, 99, 111, 134, 142, 144, 150, 157, 170, 223
Abeloe, William, 227
Alcatraz Island, 52
Alcove Springs, Kansas, 25
Alda, Nebraska, 27
Algier, Horatio, 174
Alleghany, 93
Almo, Idaho, 39
Alta California, 24, 52
Altaville, 176
Altaville Grammar School, 176
Amador City, 156
Amador County, 14, 144, 152, 153, 162
Amador County Museum, 163
Amador Hotel, 156
American Express Company, 55
American Fur Company, 33
American Hotel, 149
American Ranch, 104
American River, 12, 58
American River Inn, The, 149
American River, Middle Fork, 65, 69, 70
American River, North Fork, 65, 71
American River, South Fork, i, 12, 13, 17, 20, 23, 65
American Valley, 104
Americans, 162, 167
An Episode in Fiddletown; Harte, Bret, 154
Ancient Ruins Bluffs, 28
Angel, Henry, 177
Angels Camp, 12, 166, 177, 178, 180, 181
Angels Camp Museum, 180
Angels Creek, 174, 180
Angels Hotel, 177
Anti-Debris Act of 1883, ii
Apache (1954), 194
Apple Days, 147
Applegate (Lassen) Trail, 41
Argonaut Mine, 164
Arkansas, 31
Armstead C. Brown House, 163
Army Corps of Engineers, 208
Ash Hollow, 28
Atlantic Ocean, 48
Auburn, 12, 14, 62, 65, 66, 144
Auburn Hook and Ladder Company Fire House #2, 66
Auburn Ravine, 62, 66
Auburn's Old Town, 66
Australia, 12
Back to the Future III, 194
Bagby, 214
Bailey, Nancy Anne, 110
Balsar House, 148
Bancroft Library, i
Bancroft, Curtis, 108
Bancroft, Hubert, 109
Bancroft, Hubert Howe, 108-110
Bancroft, Louise, 108
Bank of America, 81
Bartholemew, Crowly, Empire Bakery & Restaurant, 169
Bartlett, Tom, 20
Baxter, "Buzz", 11
Bayard, Nebraska, 29, 31
Bayley House, 150
Bayley, Alcandor A., 150
Bear Flag Rebellion, 17, 24
Bear River, 81, 120, 122
Bear River Valley, Idaho, 39

Bear Valley, 215
Beckwourth Pass, 45, 111
Beckwourth Trail, 45, 111, 126
Beckwourth, James P., 24, 45, 111
Bekeart's Gunshop, 20
Bekeart, Frank, 20
Bell Store, 18
Bell Tower, 90
Bellotti's Inn, 160
Ben Hur, 218, 219
Bender, Tom, 11, 186
Bennett, Daniel, 136
Bickford, Louis, 212
Bidwell-Bartleson Party, 24, 128
Bidwell Bar, 128
Bidwell Canyon, 128
Bidwell, General John, 14, 24, 128, 132
Bidwell Mansion State Historic Park, 128
Beilharz, Alan, 227
Bierstadt, Albert, 59
Big Bar, 11
Big Country (1958), 194
Big Oak Flat, Placer County, 24
Big Oak Flat, Tuolumne County, 204
Big Sandy, 22
Bigler, David, 227
Bigler, Henry W., i, 12
Black Bart, 110, 166, 169, 170
Blair, Dr. Roger P., 25
Blue Rapids, Kansas, 25
Bodey, William S., 224
Bodie, 224-226
Bodie Cemetery, 224
Bodie State Historic Park, 224
Bok Kai Temple, 118
Boling, Captain John, 223
Bolten, Charles E., 169, 174
Bon Ton Cafe, 215
Bonanza Mine, 193
Bonnet/Compere Store, 174
Botellas, 162
Boudin's Bakery, 55
Boudin, Isadore, 55
Bourn Cottage, 78
Bowman Lake, 84, 87
Bowman Lake Dam, 87
Boy Scouts, 190
Brady Building, 189
Brannan, Sam, i, 65
Brewery Restaurant, 138
Bridgeport Covered Bridge, 82
Bridgeport Inn, 226
Bridgeport, California, 84, 226
Bridgeport, Nebraska, 28, 30
Bridger, Fort, Wyoming, 38
Bridger, Jim, 24, 38
Brignole Building, 160
Brown's Valley, 114
Brown, Alexander Stephens, i
Brown, James Stephens, i
Bryant, Edwin, 227
Budweiser Clydesdales, 178
Buffum, Edward, G., 227
Bull, Baker and Company, 134
Bungo boats, 48
Burnett, Peter, 133
Busch Building, 91
Butte City, 165
Butte County, 62, 128
Butterfield, Wasson & Company, 55
Cable Cars, 55
Cabrillo, Juan Rodriguez, 24
Cafe Max, 162
Calaveras County, 144, 166, 178, 180
Calaveras County Courthouse, 166, 169
Calaveras County Fairgrounds, 178
Calaveras County Museum and Visitors Center, 169

Calaveras Skull, The, 176
California Caverns, 170
California Centennial Commission, 14
California's Gold Rush Trail, The Traveler's Guide to; Kelly, Leslie A., 227
California Gold Rush Diary of a German Sailor, The; Windeler, Adolphus, 110, 227
California Historical Society, 14
California Militia, 128
California Overland Trail, 14, 38, 39, 41
California poppies, 13
California State Company, 115, 116
California Stage Mining and Mineral Museum, 222
California State University at Sacramento, 61
California Teacher's Association, 61
California Trail, 122
California Trail, Yesterday and Today, The; Hill, William, 227
Camino de Las Cruces, 48
Camptonville, 78, 113
Canyon Creek, 61
Canyon Creek canyon, 100
Cape Horn, 24, 46, 76, 79, 82, 128, 205
Capital Building, 60
Caribbean, 51
Carradus, Cathy, Dust Jacket, 11, 187
Carson Hill, 166, 181
Carson Pass, 4, 5, 43, 103
Carson River, 4, 5, 41, 43
Carson Sink, Nevada, 41
Carson, Kit, 24, 43
Carter House, 86
Caspar, Fort, Wyoming, 27, 33
Casper, Wyoming, 33
Cave City, 170
Cave City Caves, 170
Cedar Flat, 141
Jumping Frog of Calaveras County, The; Twain, Mark, 144, 166, 177, 178
Central Hill Channel, 173
Central Pacific Railroad, 158
Chagres, Panama, 48
Chamber of Commerce, Grass Valley, 77
Chamber of Commerce, Nevada City, 80
Chana, Claude, 62
Cheechee Flats, 171
Cherokee, 11, 12, 132
Cherokee Diggins, 132
Cherokee Indians, 132
Cherokee Mine Superintendent's house, 132
Cherokee Museum, 11, 132, 133
Chichizola Store, 164
Chico, 128
Chile, 12
Chileans, 168
Chili Gulch, 168
Chimney Point, 138
Chimney Rock, 29, 30, 31
China, 12
Chinatown, 19
Chinese, 66, 105, 126, 138, 145, 154, 168, 211, 219
Chinese Camp, 12, 200, 202
Chinese Merchant's section, 67
Chinese store, 157
Chinese Temple, 126
Cholera Epidemic, 24
Christensen, Jim "Arthritis", 11, 189
Church Street, Forest Hill, 68
Church, Methodist, Bodie, 226

Church, Methodist, Downieville, 90
Church, Serbian Orthodox, St. Sava, 165
Church, St. Ann's, 192
Church, St. Bernard's Catholic, 155
Church, St. Catherine's Catholic, 216
Church, St. Francis Xavier Catholic, 202
Church, St. James, 193
Church, St. John's Catholic, 22
Church, St. Joseph's, 163
Church, St. Joseph's Catholic, 117
Church, Sutter Creek Methodist, 158
Church, United Methodist, Jamestown, 199
City Hotel, 11, 186, 187
City Hotel, Sonora, 194
City of Gold, 126
City of Rocks, 38, 39
Clappe, Fayette, 107
Clappe, Louise Amelia Knapp Smith, 107, 109, 110
Clemens, Samuel, 166
Cleveland, Grover, 76
Coane, Kelli, 11
Cody, "Buffalo Bill", 210
Cody, Nelson, 210
Coit Tower, 53
Coit, Mrs. Lillie Hitchcock, 53
Coloma, i, 11, 12, 14, 17-19, 22, 56, 57, 65, 145, 150, 182
Coloma Cemetery, 19
Coloma County Inn, 150
Columbia, 12, 61, 182, 187, 192, 194, 198
Columbia Actor's Repertory, 188
Columbia College, 186, 188
Columbia College's Hospitality Program, 186
Columbia Firehouse #1, 184, 188
Columbia Jail House, 185
Columbia Museum, 188
Columbia School, 61
Columbia Stage Line and Stable, 11, 183
Columbia State Historic Park, 6, 7, 11, 14, 182, 183, 188
Columbia Volunteer Fire Department, 190
Columbia, Gem of the Southern Mines, 6, 7, 9, 12, 182
Comstock Mine, Nevada, 14, 80
Conestoga Wagon, 24
Congregational Church, 167
Congress, 56
Coon, Ross, 177
Cooper, Ed, 224
Cornell and Bowman Tinshop & Hardware store, 169
Cornish Christmas Celebration, 76
Cornish Miners, 76
Cornwall, England, 76
Coulter, George W., 210
Coulterville, 12, 210, 213
Coulterville Hotel, 210
Coulterville's hangin' tree, 210
Council Bluffs, Iowa, 27
Country Rose Cafe, 82
Country Store, 113
Courthouse Rock, 28, 29
Covillaud, Charles, 117
Covillaud, Mary Murphy, 117
Crabtree, Lotta, 53, 76, 82
Craycroft Building, 88
Craycroft Saloon, 88
Crimea House, 201
Crocker Art Museum, 59
Crocker, Margaret, 59

Crocker, Edwin B., 14, 59
Crotty, Tom, Suzanne, Kathleen, Kevin and Brigid, Front Cover, 11
Currier, Nathaniel, 47
Curry, Bill, 20
D'Agostini, 152
D'Agostini Winery, 152
Daffodil Hill, 157
Dame Shirley, 106, 108, 110
de Anza, Juan Bautista, 52
Deadwood, 71
Deep Ruts Hill, 32
Deer Creek, 80
Deer Creek Powerhouse, 62
Delaware River, 17
Dent, John, 208
DeSmet, Father Pierre, 34
Diamond Springs, 147
Dinkelspiel Store, 173
Dobbin's Ranch, 113
Dodge City (1939), 194
Domenghini, 169
Don Pedro Lake, 203, 234, 235
Donner Lake, 42
Donner Memorial State Park, 42
Donner Memorial State Park Museum, 42
Donner Party Rescue Site, The; Steed, Jack, 120, 227
Donner Party, 25, 38, 42, 57, 117, 120
Donner Pass, 42
Douglas Flat, 173
Downieville, 12, 88, 90, 93, 96
Drake, Sir Francis, 24
Drug Store, 86
Drum Powerhouse, 81
Drytown, 14, 156
Dughi Family, 169
Dunbar House, 175
Durst, Duane, 26
Dutch Flat, 73
Dutch Flat Bakery, 73
Dutch Flat Hotel, 73
E Clampus Vitus, 14, 86, 175, 226
E. & G. Stickle Building, 177
Eastman, H., 22
Eastwood, Clint, 194
Einfalt and Hoslinger building, 137
El Dorado Canyon, 71
El Dorado County, 18, 144, 147, 151, 222
El Dorado County Chamber of Commerce building, 144
Ellen Street, Knight's Ferry, 208
Emanuel Episcopal Church, 77
Emigrants, 26, 27, 30, 33, 34, 36-39, 111, 162
Emigration Canyon, 40
Empire Hotel, 108
Empire Mine, 78
Empire Mine State Historic Park, 78
Empire Ranch Station, 116
Emporium, 198
Engine No. 3, Sierra Railway, 200
England, 12, 24, 205
Episcopal Church, 18, 77
Eureka Mine, 78
Eureka Peak, 78
Europe, 24, 28
Europeans, 24
Evert, Grant, 178
Fairchild, John, 170
Fallon, 41
Fallon Hotel, 188
Fallon Hotel Theatre, 188
Fargo, William G., 55
Feather River, 56, 62, 108, 117, 122
Feather River, East Branch of North Fork, 106
Feather River, Middle Fork, 95, 105, 128
Feather River, North Fork, 11, 62

Fiddletown, 154
Fiddletown General Store, 154
Fielding, Karin, 212
Fippin Blacksmith Shop, 82
Firehouse #1, 80
Firehouse #2, 190
Firehouse Museum, 80
Fireman's Muster, 6, 7, 190, 191
First long distance telephone line, world's, 84
Folsom, 233
Folsom Lake State Recreation Area, 64
For Whom The Bell Tolls (1943), 194
Forbestown, 126
Forest, 93
Foresthill, 68, 70
Foresthill Cemetery, 69
Foresthill Divide, 69
Forlorn Hope Party, 120
Fort Bridger, Wyoming, 38
Fort Caspar, Wyoming, 27, 33
Fort Hall, Idaho, 39
Fort Kearny, Nebraska, 24, 26
Fort Laramie, Wyoming, 48, 49
Fort Ross, California, 56
Fort San Lorenzo, Panama, 48, 51
Fox, Dr. Kenneth, 62
Fox, P. V., 221
France, 12
Frazier, Todd, 224
French Bar, 140
French Corral, 84
French, Gulch, 134
French Hill, 167
French War, 167
Frenchtown, 115
Frémont case, 221
Frémont, General John C., 24, 215, 222
Frémont Store, 215
Fricot Nugget, 222
Frogtown, 178
Gagliardo & Company, 217
Gagliardo Store, 215
Gardella's Inn, 165
Garfield, James, 76
Garrison Family, 69
General Store, 171
Georgetown, 39, 148, 149
Georgetown Hotel, 148
Gering Valley, 29
Gering, Nebraska, 29
Gettysburg, 79
Ghirardelli Chocolate Company, 54
Ghirardelli Square, 54, 55
Ghirardelli's Chocolate Factory, 216
Ghirardelli, Domingo, 54, 216, 227
Gibson, Warren, 111
Gibsonville, 92
Gilleado Building, 173
Gillis Brothers' cabin, 192
Ginocchio Store, 165
Gold Bluffs Beach, 62, 142
Gold Discovery Journal of Azariah Smith, The; edited by Bigler, David, 227
Gold Hill, 146
Gold Hill Mine, 78
Gold Hill Mining Company, 77
Gold Lake, 62, 96, 105, 106, 142
Golden Gate Bridge, 52
Golden Gate Saloon, 76
Goldfried, Professor Howard, 61
Goodyear's Bar, 92
Goodyear's Creek, 92
Gooney's Saloon building, 169
Gorgona, Panama, 48
Graniteville, 84
Grant, Mike, 110
Grant, Norman, 108
Grant, Ulysses, 76, 174
Grass Valley, 12, 53, 74, 76, 78, 79
Grass Valley Chamber of Commerce, 77

Graton, Milton, Last of the Covered Bridge Builders, 208
Graton, Milton, New Hampshire, 208
Great Meadows, 41
Great Migration, 24
Great Salt Lake Desert, 38
Greeley, Horace, 46
Green Acres, 200
Green River, Wyoming, 38
Greenlaw, Louise, 172
Grey Eagle, 22
Grizzly Flats, 151
Grizzly Valley, 111
Grout, Ranger Sherrin N., 11, 227
Groveland, 205
Groveland Hotel, 205
Growlersburg, 148
Guernsey Ruts, 32
Guernsey, Wyoming, 32
Gunn House, 197
Gutierrez, Pablo, 120
Hall of Records, 169
Hall, Fort, Idaho, 39
Hamlet-Davis Building, 81
Hammond, Andy, 111
Hangtown, 144, 145
Hangtown Creek, 145
Hannibal, Missouri, 178
Hanover, Kansas, 26
Happy Valley, 4, 5
Harrison, Benjamin, 76
Harte, Bret, 76, 110, 154, 166, 170
Harvey, Kathi, 11, 187
Hastings, Lansford, 38
Haughin, Colin, 75
Hawaii, 12
Hayes, Lucy, 132
Hayes, Rutherford, 132
Hearst Newspapers, 171
Hearst, George, 156, 171
Hearst, William Randolph, 14, 156, 171
Heinsdorff/Thorpe Bakery building, 174
Helena, 140
Hell's Hollow, 213, 214
Henness Pass, 45
Hetch Hetchy Valley, 205
Hicks, Jr., Frank, 136
Hicks, Patricia, 136
High Noon (1952), 194
Highway 49, 14, 18, 62, 82, 92, 93, 111, 112, 144, 150, 151, 158, 165, 174, 176, 181, 210, 214
Highway 59, 209
Hildreth's Diggins, 182
Hildreth, Dr. Thadeus, 182
Hill, Thomas, 59
Hill, William E., 227
Hirschfeldter Building, 90
Historic Spots in California, Kyle, Douglas E., 227
Hock Farm, 56
Holbrooke Hotel, 76
Holle, Ronald, 26
Hollenberg Pony Express Station, 26
Hollenberg Ranch, 26
Hooterville, 200
Hoover, Herbert, 82
Hoover, Mildred Rensch, 227
Hope Valley, 43
Hornitos, 12, 54, 216
Hornitos Creek, 216
Hornitos Jail, 216
Hotel Jeffrey, 210, 211
Hotel Léger, 166, 167
Hotel Victoria, 194
Howe, John, 136
Howland Flat, 92
Hudspeth Cutoff, 39
Hughes, J. J., 34
Huie, Ranger Ken, 86
Humboldt County, 14, 142

Humboldt River, 41
Hutchings' California Magazine, 14
Hutchings, J. M., 14
Hutchinson, John, 227
Hydraulic mining, ii, 4, 132
I.O.O.F., 73, 83, 126, 216, 220
I.O.O.F. Building, 147, 162, 168, 169, 177, 204
I.O.O.F. Halls, 148
Idaho, 24, 38, 39, 41
Idaho Department of Parks and Recreation, 39
Illinois, 104
Imley, Nevada, 41
Immaculate Conception Church, 91
Independence Rock, Wyoming, 34
Independence, MO, 14, 24, 37, 46, 111
Indian Grinding Rock State Historic Park, 157
Indiana Boarding House, 108
Indians, 14, 25, 105
Iowa Hill, 72
Iron Door Saloon, 205
Isthmus Crossing, 48
Italians, 162
Italy, 12
Jackass Hill, 177, 192
Jackson, 12, 162-165
Jackson Gate, 164
Jackson, William Henry, 30, 31
Jail House Rock, 28, 29
Jamestown, 3, 12, 194, 198, 199
Jamestown Players, 3, 11, 199
Jamestown United Methodist Church, 199
Jeffrey Hotel, 210, 212
Jenny Lind, 169
Jimtown, 198
Jimtown 1849 Gold Mining Camp, 199
John Sutter's Ranch, 117
Johnson's Crossing, 24
Johnson's Rancho, 120, 122
Johnson, William, 120
Johnstun, William, i, 26
Johnsville, 99, 103
Johnsville Hotel, 103
Juanita, 88
Jumping Frog Jubilee, 178
Junction City, 138
Kaiser General Store, 155
Kansas, 26
Kearny, Fort, Nebraska, 24, 26
Kearny, General Stephen W., 24, 26, 52
Kee, Chew, 154
Kelly, Annie, 12
Kelly, Eblene, 11, 12
Kelly, Erin, 11, 109
Kelly, Patrick, Cover, 11, 170, 181
Kelsey, 22, 57
Kennebec Hill, 187, 192
Kennedy Mine, 164
Kentucky Mine Museum, 92
Keystone Mine, 156
Kidd-Knox Building, 81
Kimball, Heber C., 40
Kimmy, Norine and Brian, 44
King of Tahiti, 190
Kings Saloon, 86
Kirkwood Station, 44
Knight's Ferry, 198, 208
Knight's Ferry Covered Bridge, 208
Knowles Hill, 189
Kyle, Douglas E., 227
L. Mayor & Son building, 167
La Grange, 208, 209
La Grange Dredger, 208
La Grange Mine, 138
La Porte, 99
La Porte-Johnsville Road, 101
La Porte-Quincy Road, 100, 101
Lachman, Jimmie, 124

Lake McClure, 214
Lake Oroville, 128
Lake Spaulding, 74
Lambertville, New Jersey, 17
Laramie, Fort, Wyoming, 48, 49
    largest and richest pocket mine,
Bonanza Mine, 193
Largest gold nugget, Carson Hill, 181
Largest hydraulic gold mine, Cherokee,
    132
Lassen Trail, 96
Lassen, Peter, 134
Lawson, Pete, 3, 9, 11, 189
Lawyer's Row, 67
Lenhoff, Jim, 11, 24, 132
Lenhoff, Jim, Collection, 24
Levi Strauss & Company, 55
Levy, Joann, 227
Lewiston, 134
Lincoln Mine, 158
Lisco, Nebraska, 28
Lititz, Pennsylvania, 56
Little Mountain, 40
Livingston & Fargo, 55
Locke, Whitney, 178
Lombard Ferry, 38
Long Bar, 108
Long's Bar, 123
Longest bar, Craycroft Saloon,
    Downieville, 88
Longest covered bridge in the west,
    Knight's Ferry, 208
Longest single span covered bridge in
    the west, Bridgeport, 82
Los Angeles, 17, 24
Lott, C. F., House, 126
Lotta's Fountain, 53
Lotus, 150
Luck of Roaring Camp, The; Harte,
    Bret, 110
Macy's Store, 117
Macy, Rowland H., 14, 177
Magnolia Saloon, 212
Main Street, Columbia, 189
Main Street, Hornitos, 216
Major, Colonel Richard B., 22, 144
Malakoff Diggins, 12, 84, 86, 87
Malakoff Diggins State Historic Park,
    ii, 14, 85, 86
Man Lee Store, 19
Mariposa, 12, 182, 210, 220, 222
Mariposa Battalion, 144, 223
Mariposa County, 10, 14, 144, 210,
    213, 219, 221, 222
Mariposa County Courthouse, 1, 215,
    221
Mariposa County Fairgrounds, 222
Mariposa Creek, 220
Mariposa Gazette, The, 221
Mariposa Mining Company, 215
Mariposa Museum and History Center,
    222
Marshall, 150
Marshall Gold Discovery State Historic
    Park, Cover, i, 11, 17,
    18, 20, 21
Marshall, James W., i, 13, 14, 17, 19,
    22, 56, 57, 65, 70, 80,150
Mary Aaron Museum, 117
Mary Harrison Mine, 210
Marysville, 12, 44, 99, 111, 116, 117
Marysville, Town of, 117
Marysville-La Porte Road, 114, 115
Masonic Building, Nevada City, 81
Masonic Building, Hornitos, 216
Masonic Hall, Columbia, 188
Masonic Lodge, Shasta, 134
Massachusetts, 110
Mattison Mine, 176
McAdams Store, 202
McCarthy's store, 210
McClintock, Delia, 224

McCormick, Kevin, 111
McHenry, Chief Ranger Rosanne N.,
    Cover, 11
McLaughlin, 157
Meeker, Ezra, 37
Merced River, 214, 223
Methodist Church, Bodie, 226
Methodist Church, Downieville, 90
Mexican Bandit, Joaquin Murieta, 169,
    216
Mexican War, 17, 26
Mexicans, 17, 162, 193, 212
Mexico, 12, 24, 52
Michigan Bluff, 70, 71
Milton Mining and Water Company, 84
Miraflores Locks, Panama Canal, 50
Missions, 24
Mississippi River, 1, 221
Missouri, 14, 154
Missouri River, 24
Mitchell Pass, 29
Moccasin Creek, 205, 206
Moccasin Point, 228
Moccasin Powerhouse, 205, 206
Modesto Irrigation District, 203
Mokelumne Hill, 12, 166, 168
Mokelumne River, 11, 165
Monk, Hank, 55
Mono County Courthouse, 226
Monte Cristo Mine, 104
Monterey, 24
Monterey Colonial Architectural Style,
    205
Montez, Lola, 77, 81, 82
Monumental Quartz Mine, 91
Morgan, Henry, 51
Mormon Bar, 222
Mormon Battalion, i, 12, 43, 44, 56,
    222
Mormon Cabin, 19
Mormon Church, I,
Mormon Emigrants, 27, 28, 33, 38, 40
Mormon Island, i, 65
Mormon Trail, 40, 43, 44
Mormon War, 38
Mormons, 65
Morrison, Tracy, Back Cover
Mother Lode Country, 14
Mount, William, 46
Mountain House, 126
Mountain Messenger, The, 90
Mountain Ranch, 169, 178
Mountains of California; Muir, John,
    170
Mt. Aukom, 151
Muir, John, 170
Murietta, Joaquin, 169, 216
Murphy, Daniel, 174
Murphy, John, 174
Murphy, Mary, 120
Murphys, 12, 174, 175
Murphys Diggins, 174
Murphys Flat, 174
Murphys Hotel, 174
Murray, Tom, 224
Nahl, Charles Christian, 59
Natchez, The, riverboat, 46
National Frontier Trails Center, 24
National Gold Panning Championship,
    20
National Hotel, Jackson, 162
National Hotel, Jamestown, 198
National Hotel, Nevada City, 82
National Register of Historic Places,
    136
Native Daughters of the Golden West,
    14
Native Sons of the Golden West, 14, 67
Nebraska, 28, 29
Nebraska State Historical Society, 31
Nelson Creek, 105
Nelson's Point, 105

Nevada crossing, 24
Nevada (County) Irrigation District, 74,
    116
Nevada City, California, 12, 62, 80
Nevada City, Nevada, 14, 81
Nevada County, 12, 62, 74, 81, 84, 86
Nevada County Historical Mining
    Museum, 78
Nevada Theatre, 80
New England, 68, 157
New Helvetia, 14, 56
New Melones Reservoir, 181
New Orleans, 46
New York, 24, 46, 47
New York Daily Tribune, 46
New York Saturday Press, 178
Newtown, 151
Nombre de Díos, Panama, 48
North America, 62
North Bloomfield, 84, 86
North Bloomfield ditch, 87
North Bloomfield Gravel Mining
    Company, 87
North Columbia School, 85
North Platte, 27, 33
North San Juan, 84, 85
North Star Mine, 78
North, Julius, 134
Northern Mariposa County History
    Center, 210, 211
Northern Mines, 14, 62, 73, 77, 78,
    113, 126, 144, 177
Norway, 103
O'Shaughnessy Dam, 205
Oklahoma, 132
Old Costa Store, 172
Old Dry Diggins, 145
Old Eureka Mine, 158
Old General Store at Forest Hill, 69
Old Monumental, 184, 190
Old Pacific Brewery Building, 138
Old Sacramento, 58, 59
Old Stone Store at Dutch Flat, 73
Old Town Auburn, 67
Old-Timers Museum, 175
Oldest continuous operating hotel,
    National Hotel, Nevada City, 82
Oldest courthouse in continuous use,
    Mariposa, 221
Oldest drugstore, Weaverville, 136
Oldest post office, Auburn, 66
Oldest Protestant church in continuous
    use, Downieville, 90
Oldest repertory Theatre, Nevada City,
    80
Oldest saloon in continuous operation,
    Golden Gate Saloon, 76
Oldest saloon, Iron Door Saloon, 205
Oldest weekly newspaper, The
    Mountain Messenger, 90
Oldfield, Crystal, 178
Olmstead, Frederick Law, 215
Omaha World-Herald Quesenbury
    Sketchbook, 31
Onion Valley, 100
Ophir City, 126
Oregon, 17, 24, 37
Oregon-California Trail Association,
    111
Oregon City, 133
Oregon City School, 133
Oregon Creek Covered Bridge, 112
Oregon Trail, 24, 30, 37, 39
Oregon-California Trail, 26, 27, 28, 30,
    36, 39
Oregon-California Trail Association, 44
Original 16-1 Mine, 93
Oroville, 12, 126, 128, 130, 132
Oroville Dam, 128
Oroville Lake Project, 128
Orick, 143
Osborn, Ford, 111

Ott, J. J., Assay Office, 80
Outcasts of Poker Flat, The; Harte,
    Bret, 110
Overland Trails, 196
P & L Mercantile, 114
Pacific Gas and Electric Company, 62,
    81, 82
Pacific Ocean, 142
Pacific Springs, 36
Pacific Steamship Lines, 51
Palace Restaurant, 161
Panama, 12, 48, 49, 50, 51
Panama Canal Commission, 48, 51
Panama City, 48, 50, 51
Panama Isthmus, 14, 24, 46, 48
Panama Viejo, 51
Papeete, 190
Parque Nacional de Soberanía, 48
Pasties, 76
Pelton Water Wheel, 78, 81, 113
Pelton, Lester Allen, 78, 113
Peru, 12, 54
Peter L. Traver Building, 175
Piety Hill, Sonora, 193, 197
Pilot Hill, 150
Pilot Peak, 99, 100
Pine Grove, 157
Pioneer 157
Pioneer Cemetery, 218
Pioneer Hotel, 171
Pioneer Monument, 42
Pioneer, The, 110
Placer County, 64
Placer County Chamber of Commerce,
    66
Placer County Courthouse, 66
Placerville, 12, 61, 144, 145, 147, 182
Platte River, 27, 28
Plaza, Hornitos, 216
Pleasant Valley, 151
Pliocene Ridge, 93
Plumas-Eureka Mine, 102, 103
Plumas-Eureka State Park, 102, 103
Plumas County Museum, 105
Plumas County Sheriff's Department,
    110
Plumas National Forest, 104
Plymouth, 152, 157
Pocatello, Idaho, 39
Poker Flat, Sierra Country, 61, 100
Pokerville, 157
Polk, James K., 24, 46
Pony Express, 59
Port Wine, 92
Port Wine Store, 92
Prairie Creek Redwood State Park, 143
Pralle, Rick, 26
Presidio de San Francisco, 52
Pride of San Joaquin, 178
Prince and Garibardi Building, 176
Quartzburg, 216
Queen City, 92
Queensbury, William, 31
Quick Ranch, 219
Quincy, 12, 99, 104, 105
Rackerby Stage Stop, 114
Raft River, 39
Raggio Family, 169
Railtown 1897, 200
Rancho las Mariposas, 215
Readings' Springs, 134
Red Bluff, 134
Red Church, 193
Red Lake, 43
Reno, Nevada, 45
Rensch, Ethel Grace, 227
Rensch, Hero Eugene, 227
Rich Bar, 11, 106, 107, 108, 109, 110
Rich Bar Mining Company, 108
Richest and roughest mining camp,
    Hornitos, 216
Richest river bar, Rich Bar, 108

Río Chagres, 48
Robinson's Ferry, 181
Rocky Mountains, 33
Romaggi House, 181
Rose, Violet, 170
Rosenberger, Dave, 224
Ross, Fort, California, 56
Rough and Ready, 53, 82, 83, 122
Rough and Ready Riders, 122
Roughing It; Twain, Mark, 55
Royce, Josiah, 110
Rubicon River, 70
Sacramento, 12, 20, 22, 56, 58, 59, 62, 120
Sacramento River, 58, 134
Sacramento, State Capital of California, 60
Salt Lake Alternate Trail, 39
Salt Lake City, 27, 33, 38, 40, 43
San Andreas, 12, 167, 169
San Diego, 24
San Francisco, i, 14, 24, 46, 47, 52, 55, 65, 110, 134, 182, 203, 205, 216
San Francisco County, 203
San Francisco Harbor, 190
San Francisco Mint, 52
San Francisco, Port of, 52
San José, 24, 44
San Juan Channel, 84
San Juan Ridge, 84
San Lorenzo, Fort, Panama, 48, 51
San Rafael, 17
Sand Pond, 94
Sandwich Islands, 12
Sank Park, 126
Santa Barbara, 24
Sardine Lake, 98
Savage, Major James D., 44, 210, 223
Sawyer Decision, January 23, 1884, ii, 84, 86
Sawyer, Tom, 178
Schallorn Building, 154
Schlageter Hotel, 220
Scotts Bluff, Nebraska, 28-30
Scotts Bluff National Monument, 29
Serbian Orthodox Church of St. Sava, 165
Serbians, 162
Shasta, 122, 134, 136
Shasta City, 134
Shasta County, 62
Shasta County Courthouse, 8
Shasta State Historic Park, 8, 134
Shasta, Queen City of the Northern Mines, 8
Sheep Ranch, 171
Sheep Ranch Mine, 171
Shenandoah Valley, 152, 153
Shenandoah Vineyards, 152
Sheridan, Wyoming, 24
Sherman, General W. T., 132
Shirley Letters, The; Clappe, Louise, 227
Shirley, Dame a.k.a. Louise Clappe, 106, 108-110
Shirt Tail Canyon, 70
Shriver, A. F., 221
Sierra Buttes, 91, 92, 94
Sierra City, 91
Sierra County, 61, 62, 88, 92, 96
Sierra Nevada, 84, 103, 111, 120, 122, 136, 196
Sierra Nevada House, 150
Sierra Nevada Mountains, 12, 25, 41, 42, 45
Sierra Railway, 200
Sierra Valley, 96, 111
Sikes, Nanci, 11
Silva, Kimberly, 116
Silver Dollar Saloon, 118
Silver Lake, 44

Six Months in the Gold Fields, Buffum, Edward, G., 227
Smartville, 116
Smartville Cemetery, 116
Smith, Azariah, I,
Smith, Jedediah Strong, 24
Snake River, 39
Sobon, Lee, 152
Sobon Vineyards, 152
Soda Springs, 39
Sonoma, 24
Sonora, 6, 7, 12, 193, 194, 208
Sonora Herald, 197
Sonora Inn, 194
Sonora Pass, 45
Sonora, Mexico, 216
Sonora, Queen of the Southern Mines, 193
Sonorian Camp, 193
South America, 24
South Pass, 45
South Yuba Canal, 74
Southern Mines, 14, 144, 166, 216
Spain, 24, 48, 51
Spaniards, 51
Spanish, 24
Spanish Creek, 104
Spanish Peak, 104
Spanish Ranch, 104
Sperry and Perry's Hotel, 174
Spider Dance, 77, 81
Spring Valley Hydraulic Gold Company, 132
Spring Valley Mine, 12, 132
Spring Valley Mine and Assay Office, 133
St. Ann's Church, 192
St. Bernard's Catholic Church, 155
St. Catherine's Catholic Church, 216
St. Charles Inn, 92
St. Francis Xavier Catholic Church, 202
St. George Hotel, 155
St. James Church, 193
St, John's Catholic Church, 22
St. Joseph's Catholic Church, 117
St. Joseph's Church, 220
St. Patrick's Catholic Church, 163
Standard Mine, 225
Stanford University, 71, 158
Stanford, Leland J., 14, 71, 158
Stanislaus County, 208
Stanislaus River, 169, 181, 208
State Department of Water Resources, 128
State Historic Park, Bidwell Mansion, 128
State Historic Park, Bodie, 224
State Historic Park, Columbia, 6, 7, 11, 14, 182, 183, 188
State Historic Park, Donner Lake, 42
State Historic Park, Empire Mine, 78, 79
State Historic Park, Indian Grinding Rock, 157
State Historic Park, Malakoff Diggins, ii, 14, 85, 86
State Historic Park, Marshall Gold Discovery, i, 11, 17, 18, 20, 21
State Historic Park, Shasta, 8, 134
State Historic Park, Sutter's Fort, 22, 56, 57
State Historic Park, Weaverville Joss House, 138
State Park, Donner Memorial, 42
State Park, Plumas-Eureka, 102, 103
Steed, Jack, 120, 122
Steiner, Stan, 190
Stockton, 208
Stoddart, 96
Stoller, Davy, 11
Strauss, Levi, 14, 55

Street-Morgan Mansion, 197
Studebaker Company, 145
Studebaker, Clement, 145
Studebaker, Henry, 145
Studebaker, John Mohler, 14, 145
Sublette, William, 34
Sucker Flat, 116
Sugar Loaf Mountain, 132
Sugarman, Superintendent Matt, 11
Sun Sun Wo Company, 211
Sutter Buttes, 123, 124
Sutter County, 123
Sutter Creek, 12, 158, 160
Sutter Creek Inn, 160
Sutter Creek Methodist Church, 158
Sutter's Fort, 56-58, 122
Sutter's Fort State Historic Park, 22, 56, 57
Sutter's Hock Farm, 125
Sutter's Mill, i, 1, 14, 19, 22, 56
Sutter, John Augustus, 14, 17, 19, 56, 65, 120, 125, 158
Sutter, Jr., John Augustus, 58
Sweetwater River, 34
Switzerland, 56, 58
Table Mountain, Butte County, 126, 130, 132
Table Mountain, Tuolumne County, 198, 201
Táboga Island, 51
Taylor, Bayard, 48
Telegraph Hill, 52
Temple Amongst the Forest Beneath the Clouds, Weaverville, 138
Temple, Bok Kai, Marysville, 117
Temple, Chinese, Oroville, 127
Thatcher, Becky, 178
The Great American West, 194
The Red Glove, 194
The Virginian (1924), 194
They Saw the Elephant, Women in the California Gold Rush; Levy, Joann, 227
This Is The Place Monument, 40
Thompson Building, 175
Thompson, John "Snowshoe", 103
Thorn, B. K., 170
Timbuctoo, 61, 116
Tinnin Building, 137
Tioga Pass, 45
Tong War, 138
Trading Post Cafe, 75
Trading Post, 208
Tragedy Springs, 44
Traveling California's Gold Rush Country; Kelly, Leslie A., 227
Tremoureux House, 79
Trinity County, 62
Trinity County Courthouse, 136
Trinity Journal, the, 137
Trinity Mountains, 136
Trinity River, 138, 140, 141
Truckee, 42
Truckee River, 38, 41
Tucker, Silas, 134
Tuolumne County, 3, 12, 144, 177, 194, 228
Tuolumne County Museum, 196
Tuolumne County Visitors Bureau, 11
Tuolumne County Visitors Bureau, Chinese Camp, 202
Tuolumne River, 208, 209
Turlock Irrigation District, 203
Tuttletown, 12
Twain, Mark, 55, 76, 166, 170, 174, 177, 178, 192
Twin Sisters Rock, 39
Tyson, Ed, 81
Uinta Mountains, 38
Unforgiven, 194
Union Hotel, Kelsey, 22
Union Hotel, La Porte, 99

Union Jack, 75
United Methodist Church, Jamestown, 199
Universal Pictures, 194
Utica Mine, 177
Vallecito, 173
Valley of the Great Salt Lake, 40
Vassaelo/Ruiseco & Orengo/Segale Store, 174
Ventura, Bill, 11
Venus, 214
Vinton, 111
Virginiatown, 61
Vizcaíno, Sebastián, 24
Volcano, 155, 157
Wah Hop, 19
Walker River Route, 45
Walker, Joseph Reddeford, 24, 45
Wall of Comparative Ovations of E Clampus Vitus, 175
Walters, Fred, 138
Ward, Linda, 224
Wasatch Mountains, 38
Washington, 75
Washington Street, Sonora, 194, 197
Washington, D.C., 56
Washington, George, 17
Washoe Lake, Nevada, 80
Way, Jane, 160
Weaver, John, 136
Weaverville, 12, 122, 136, 138
Weaverville Drugstore, 136
Weaverville Joss House State Historic Park, 138
Wells & Company, 55
Wells, Fargo & Company, 55, 61, 84, 91, 116, 148, 168, 182, 184, 202, 210, 215
Wells, Henry, 55
Western Star Number Two, 134
What Cheer House, 186
What I Saw in California; Bryant, Edwin, 227
Wheatland, 24, 122
Whistling Billy, 210
Wild West Film Fest, Tuolumne County, 194
Williamette Valley, 39
Wimmer Nugget, I,
Wimmer, Mrs., I,
Wind River Range, 36
Windeler, Adolphus, 110, 227
Windlass Hill, 28
Winkler Store, 169
Won Lim Miao, 138
Wood's Creek, Jamestown, 199
Wood's Crossing, 3
Wood's Dry Diggins, 66
Woodleaf Hotel, 115
Woodruff, Wilford, 40
Woods, Monica, 20
Woodville House, 115
World Rushed In, The; Holiday, J. S., 227
Wyoming, 32, 33, 36
YB34, 74
Yee, 154
Yerba Buena, 47, 52
Yosemite, 210, 223
Yosemite National Park, 144

The Meadow Creek Ranch Bed and Breakfast, south of
Mariposa on Highway 49, was originally a stage stop when
built in 1858. The comfortable sleeping rooms and dining and
sitting areas provide hospitality in the tradition of California's
gold rush era.

The Wells Fargo and Company Building at Folsom, built in 1860, is one of a number of remaining structures from the gold rush era on Sutter Street. The site of Folsom on the American River, first known as Negro Bar, was mined by Blacks from 1849. Folsom became an important transportation center for both stage coach and freight services.

Postword

A solitary jet skier creates figure eights on Don Pedro Lake, as seen here from Moccasin Point in Tuolumne County. During California's gold rush era, miners lined the rivers and streams of California's gold rush country seeking "the color." Today, residents and visitors line the banks or use boats and personal water craft to enjoy many recreational opportunities found in and along the lakes and rivers of California's gold rush country.

There are many reminders of California's gold rush for visitors to explore and marvel at on the occasion of the Sesquicentennial Anniversary. Preservationists are hard at work to protect many of the old buildings and sites to help future generations understand the historic significance of California's gold rush. The State of California, through the